## HENRIK IBSEN

Born in Norway in 1828, Henrik Ibsen began his writing career
with romantic history plays influenced by Shakespeare and
Schiller. In 1851 he was appointed writer-in-residence at the
newly established Norwegian Theatre in Bergen with a contract
to write a play a year for five years, following which he was
made Artistic Director of the Norwegian Theatre in what is now
Oslo. In the 1860s he moved abroad to concentrate wholly on
writing. He began with two mighty verse dramas, *Brand* and
*Peer Gynt*, and in the 1870s and 1880s wrote the sequence of
realistic 'problem' plays for which he is best known, among them
*A Doll's House*, *Ghosts*, *An Enemy of the People*, *Hedda Gabler*
and *Rosmersholm*. His last four plays, *The Master Builder*, *Little
Eyolf*, *John Gabriel Borkman* and *When We Dead Awaken*, dating
from his return to Norway in the 1890s, are increasingly overlaid
with symbolism. Illness forced him to retire in 1900, and he died
in 1906 after a series of crippling strokes.

## CORDELIA LYNN

Cordelia Lynn is a playwright and librettist. Plays include an adaptation of Anton Chekhov's *Three Sisters* (Almeida Theatre); *One For Sorrow*, *Lela & Co.* (Royal Court Theatre); *Best Served Cold* (VAULT Festival). Opera includes *Miranda* (Opéra Comique). Other vocal work includes *Heave* (Festival Royaumont); *The White Princess* (Festival d'Aix-en-Provence); *you'll drown, dear* (Festival Manifest). Dramaturgy includes *Lucia di Lammermoor* (Royal Opera House). Cordelia was awarded the Harold Pinter Commission in 2017 and is a MacDowell Colony fellow, 2018.

Cordelia Lynn

# HEDDA TESMAN

*After Henrik Ibsen*

## NICK HERN BOOKS

London

www.nickhernbooks.co.uk

**A Nick Hern Book**

*Hedda Tesman* first published as a paperback original in Great Britain in 2019 by Nick Hern Books Limited, The Glasshouse, 49a Goldhawk Road, London W12 8QP, in association with Headlong Theatre, Chichester Festival Theatre and The Lowry

*Hedda Tesman* copyright © 2019 Cordelia Lynn

Cordelia Lynn has asserted her right to be identified as the author of this version

Cover photography by The Other Richard; cover design by Sean Longmore at The Lowry

Designed and typeset by Nick Hern Books, London
Printed in Great Britain by Mimeo Ltd, Huntingdon, Cambridgeshire PE29 6XX

A CIP catalogue record for this book is available from the British Library

ISBN    978 1 84842 895 9

*Hedda Tesman* was first produced by Chichester Festival Theatre, Headlong and The Lowry, and first performed at the Minerva Theatre, Chichester, on 30 August 2019. The cast was as follows:

| | |
|---|---|
| HEDDA TESMAN | Haydn Gwynne |
| GEORGE TESMAN | Anthony Calf |
| BERTHA | Rebecca Oldfield |
| JULIE TESMAN | Jacqueline Clark |
| THEA TESMAN | Natalie Simpson |
| BRACK | Jonathan Hyde |
| ELIJAH | Irfan Shamji |
| PIANISTS | Catriona Beveridge |
| | Jennifer Whyte |

| | |
|---|---|
| *Director* | Holly Race Roughan |
| *Designer* | Anna Fleischle |
| *Lighting Designer* | Zoe Spurr |
| *Music* | Ruth Chan |
| *Sound Designer* | George Dennis |
| *Casting Director* | Charlotte Sutton |

## Hauntings: Author's Note

*Hedda Tesman* is a modern adaptation of Henrik Ibsen's *Hedda Gabler*, from a literal translation by Anne-Marie Stanton-Ife. The idea was to create a piece of new writing held within Ibsen's original play. Careful attention was paid to his structure, story, form, tone and symbolism. As a way of addressing developments in socio-political conditions for women since 1891, the ages and relationships of some of the characters have been changed.

An adaptation is a haunted thing. *Hedda Tesman* is perhaps more haunted than some. I think this is why the house in the play became a haunted house, lived in by a haunted woman. The past always surfaces, like a ghost.

I am thankful to Holly Race Roughan, without whom *Hedda Tesman* would and could not have been written.

*C.L.*

## Characters

HEDDA TESMAN, *born Gabler, early sixties*
GEORGE TESMAN, *Hedda's husband, a historian, early sixties*
BERTHA, *a cleaner, mid-thirties*
JULIE TESMAN, *George's aunt, mid-eighties*
THEA TESMAN, *Hedda and George's daughter, late twenties*
BRACK, *Hedda and George's friend, mid-sixties*
ELIJAH, *former student of George's, early thirties*

## Scene

An isolated house, outside a university town.

Today, now.

## Notes

*The House* indicates The House making itself known.

A forward slash (/) indicates an external interruption.

A dash (–) indicates an internal interruption.

An ellipsis (…) indicates a tailing-off.

*This text went to press before the end of rehearsals and so may differ slightly from the play as performed.*

## ACT ONE

*A house. Dark. Sense of morning.*

*Someone trying to get in.*

*Front door opens.*

*Thump.*

BERTHA (*off*). Shit!

> *Beat.*

> (*Soft, off.*) Hello?

> *Beat.*

> *Footsteps. Not carpet.*

> *Lights on. Tungsten bulb. Gold and dim. Shadows.*

> *Large kitchen. Old. Decaying. Ugly. A stove, wood burning. Incongruously, a piano. Large shuttered doors leading to a garden. The doors are open.*

> *Further in the house, a sitting room. A mantelpiece. Above the mantelpiece a portrait of a general.*

> *Everywhere boxes. A life to be unwrapped.*

> *Dreadful wallpaper.*

BERTHA *in the kitchen doorway. Hand on light switch.*

> *Beat.*

BERTHA *to the garden doors.*

> (*Into the garden.*) Hello-o?

> *Beat.*

*Exit* BERTHA, *hallway.*

*A light breeze.*

*Enter* BERTHA *with cleaning materials. Looks around the kitchen.*

*Sighs.*

*Opens a cardboard box and unpacks it. One by one unwraps things from packing paper, puts them on the table. Hums as she works.*

*A large rectangular case in bubble wrap. Removes the bubble wrap. Wipes down the case. Opens the case.*

*Stops humming.*

*Beat.*

*Looks around.*

*Carefully lifts a Second World War service revolver out of the case.*

*Stares at it.*

*Takes out another, its twin.*

*Stares at them.*

*Beat.*

*Aims the guns.*

Bang ba-da bang bang!

*Lowers the guns. Looks around. Sees The General through the doorway.*

(*American accent.*) There ain't enough space in this town for the two of us.

*The General doesn't respond.*

*Beat.*

*Draws the guns at The General.*

Bang Bang!

*Blows smoke from the barrels.*

*The House.*

*Puts the guns back in the case and closes it.*

*Unwraps a music box. Opens the lid.*

*'Hush little baby' plays.*

*Enter* GEORGE, *garden door.*

GEORGE. Morning!

BERTHA. Oh!

*Shuts the music box.*

You scared me /

GEORGE. Sorry! You must be…

The cleaner.

BERTHA. Bertha.

GEORGE. Bertha, hello. George Tesman.

*Beat.*

Bertha. That's a nice name.

BERTHA. No it's not.

*Beat.*

I mean /

GEORGE. Well yes.

*Beat.*

Thanks for coming so early /

BERTHA. Well they said to. But I'll come when you like, if you let me know. Or the agency. Let them know /

GEORGE. It's just while we're settling in, then the hours will be more reasonable.

BERTHA *unpacking the box.*

BERTHA. They said to do the unpacking, said you'd been away.

GEORGE. Just got back. Best keep it down actually, Hedda's sleeping.

BERTHA. Hedda?

GEORGE. My wife.

BERTHA. Where were you?

GEORGE. Boston.

BERTHA. I've never been to Boston.

GEORGE. Neither had I until we moved there.

BERTHA. What were you doing?

GEORGE. I had a job for a few years, a fellowship.

BERTHA. Doing what?

GEORGE. I'm a historian.

*Beat.*

BERTHA. Cool.

GEORGE. I think it is –

Ah!

*The music box.*

I haven't seen this for years…

*Opens the lid.*

*'Hush little baby' plays.*

*It winds down.*

*Pause.*

That belonged to my daughter.

BERTHA. She live here too?

GEORGE. No. No she –

Well I think she lives in London.

*Beat.*

I'd hoped these would have got lost in storage…

*Touches the gun case.*

BERTHA. Yeah. So

the guns /

GEORGE. You opened it?

*Beat.*

Best not. Hedda's rather attached to them.

BERTHA. Your wife?

GEORGE. They were her father's. He was in the army.

BERTHA. So was mine!

*Beat.*

I don't have any guns though.

GEORGE. He was a general.

BERTHA. My dad wasn't a general.

GEORGE. He was older, served in the Second World War.

BERTHA. Wow.

GEORGE. Yes, he inspired 'wow' in people…

BERTHA. Was he nice?

GEORGE. Nice? (*Laughs.*) Well… Hedda adored him but I didn't really know him. Died shortly before we were married.

There.

*The General.*

General Gabler.

BERTHA. Watching over you.

GEORGE. I suppose he's not going to leave us alone…

*A key in the front-door lock.*

*They are very still.*

*Front door.*

*Shuffling in the hallway.*

*Stop.*

JULIE (*off*). Suitcases.

GEORGE. Auntie Julie?

*Exit* GEORGE.

(*Off.*) Auntie Julie!

JULIE (*off*). Dearest boy! Welcome back!

GEORGE (*off*). Watch the bags…

GEORGE *and* JULIE *in the kitchen.* JULIE *has flowers.*

JULIE. Well this is very nice! Your new home!

GEORGE. Lovely flowers, there'll be a vase somewhere…

JULIE. Oh hello dear…

BERTHA. Hi.

GEORGE. Bertha, my aunt, Julie /

JULIE. But everyone calls me Auntie Julie.

BERTHA. Hello

Auntie Julie.

JULIE. She got the keys then. I arranged it all with the agency but you never know.

GEORGE. Thanks so much for overseeing the move.

JULIE. You know I like to be helpful. Is everything as it should be?

GEORGE. Just the boxes to arrive from America now /

*Snap.*

BERTHA. Sorry.

*BERTHA is folding the cardboard box.*

I'll leave you both to it and start on the hoovering /

JULIE. Don't mind me dear /

BERTHA. It's fine I'll /

JULIE. You do whatever you think is best /

BERTHA. Right so /

JULIE. We should all be completely at home!

*Beat.*

BERTHA. So I'll just go and do that.

GEORGE. Thanks Bertha.

*Exit BERTHA with box and paper.*

JULIE. What a nice girl. Auntie Rina and I have always preferred to do our own cleaning of course but I do understand that for Hedda...

GEORGE. How is Auntie Rina?

JULIE. As well as can be expected.

GEORGE. I'll come round as soon as we're settled.

JULIE. She's so looking forward to seeing you. She missed you so much...

GEORGE. Let me take those... Nice hat! Is it new?

JULIE. Very new! I bought it specially.

GEORGE. Specially?

JULIE. Now that you're back I thought Hedda might like to go on some little trips with me.

GEORGE. Little trips?

JULIE. To galleries and museums, National Trust houses...

GEORGE. I'm sure she'd love to.

JULIE. But you know Hedda, always so stylish. I wouldn't want to look like an old frump next to her.

GEORGE. It'll be nice for her, something to keep her occupied anyway.

JULIE. That's what I thought... But I want to hear all about America. Was it productive?

GEORGE. Did you see the suitcases in the hall? The big one near the door?

JULIE. See it? I nearly fell over it!

GEORGE. Guess what it's full of.

*Beat.*

JULIE. Clothes.

GEORGE. Notes! Hundreds of pages of notes. The archives out there, it's amazing.

JULIE. And what's your next masterpiece to be on?

GEORGE. I'm going for something a little more specialist this time.

JULIE. Yes?

GEORGE. Domestic Crafts in the Medieval Brabant.

*Beat.*

JULIE. You're so clever! How do you even come across these things?

GEORGE. I suppose I find them interesting.

JULIE. And did Hedda have a nice time?

GEORGE. Oh yes. She organised lots of

things. You know, parties and things.

JULIE. She must be very disappointed to come back.

GEORGE. I don't know... I don't think so. It's hard to tell with Hedda.

JULIE. It is hard to tell with Hedda.

*They laugh. They have often laughed about Hedda, over the years.*

And now! You're going to be a professor!

GEORGE. It's not official yet.

JULIE. They must have been keen not to let you get away from them back here.

GEORGE. You think so?

JULIE. After the success of your last book...

GEORGE. This is where my heart is. I've spent my life at this university.

JULIE. It's your home.

GEORGE. And Hedda's.

*Beat.*

JULIE. Where is she?

GEORGE. Sleeping.

JULIE. Sleeping!

GEORGE. We don't all have your energy /

JULIE. Actually I'm glad she's asleep. I wanted to talk to you alone.

GEORGE. Is everything alright?

JULIE. Thea's back George.

*Beat.*

She came back yesterday.

GEORGE. Right.

*Beat.*

What do you mean?

JULIE. She says she needs to stay for a few days /

GEORGE. Is she in trouble?

JULIE. She's fine, you mustn't worry /

GEORGE. I am worrying.

JULIE. But you mustn't, which is why I thought I'd let you know before she comes /

GEORGE. She's coming here?

JULIE. She said she needed to speak to you.

GEORGE. But we haven't seen her for, what? Five years? And now without any warning, without /

JULIE. You know I don't like to interfere /

GEORGE. She expressly forbade any contact /

JULIE. But what if this were an opportunity to –

GEORGE (*soft*). Auntie Julie...

JULIE. Your daughter, George. Your and Hedda's /

GEORGE. Best leave this to me, with Hedda I mean. She's still a little

fragile.

It's not that I don't appreciate everything you're doing and everything you did. For Thea.

JULIE. What else could I have done? She needed looking after and you've always worked so hard. And it's not as though her mother /

GEORGE. Yes.

JULIE. It was hard on you.

GEORGE. I'm lucky to have Hedda.

*Beat.*

I still wake up in the morning sometimes and wonder what she's doing there next to me.

And then. Thirty years...

JULIE. You love her so much.

GEORGE. And now I can finally give her the home she wanted. Ever since we were first married she wanted to live in this house.

HEDDA *in the doorway, pyjamas and dressing gown. Watches them.*

We're going to retire here. We'll plant fruit trees in the garden. Hedda can make jam.

I can't think of anything nicer than home-made jam for breakfast /

HEDDA. George there's a strange woman wandering around our house with a hoover.

GEORGE. You're up!

JULIE. Welcome home Hedda!

*Goes to her.*

HEDDA *flinches.*

JULIE *stops.*

HEDDA. Hello Julia. Sorry, I'm a bit

tired.

JULIE. We didn't disturb you did we?

HEDDA. No.

Yes. Well it wasn't you. It's the silence out here it's

deafening.

GEORGE. But you always said you wanted somewhere quiet /

HEDDA. Did I?

GEORGE. And she slept like a log on the plane /

HEDDA. I have never in my life done anything like a log –

Oh why is it so bright in here!

JULIE. Well it is morning.

HEDDA. It's like everything's on fire…

GEORGE. We'll close the shutters.

HEDDA. What's all this on the –

Flowers.

GEORGE. Auntie Julie brought them. Isn't that sweet?

HEDDA. To come so early and bring flowers. You really
shouldn't have.

JULIE. And I have another present.

GEORGE. You're spoiling us! Isn't she spoiling us Hedda?

HEDDA. Yes. She is.

JULIE. It's just a small thing…

*A present, wrapped, from her bag.*

GEORGE. Would you like to open it Hedda?

HEDDA. I'm okay /

JULIE. Yes you open it Hedda /

HEDDA. I really /

JULIE. It would make me so happy if you opened it.

*Beat.*

HEDDA *opens the present.*

HEDDA. It's a

lovely… /

GEORGE. Photograph album!

*Takes it, opens it.*

HEDDA *to shutters, looks out through the slats. Bars of light on her.*

All our pictures from America!

JULIE. We thought it would be nice for you to have them in one place.

GEORGE. Isn't it nice Hedda?

JULIE. Auntie Rina put it together, you know how clever she is.

GEORGE. Ah there's our little house…

JULIE. Such a sweet little house.

GEORGE. And here's that party you threw Hedda, for the whole faculty. Wasn't that fun?

JULIE. It looks fun!

GEORGE. There's the Dean. And his wife. Such a clever man. There I am with the Vice Chancellor, and his wife. And there's that lovely woman, what was she…

Junior Lecturer in…

HEDDA. The War of Independence.

GEORGE. But where's Hedda?

HEDDA. At the back probably.

GEORGE. There you are! Doesn't she look beautiful?

HEDDA. Don't George /

JULIE. Very beautiful /

HEDDA. Please /

JULIE. Such a stylish dress. I couldn't have pulled it off at her age /

GEORGE. Rubbish /

JULIE. It's the arms, you see. A woman's arms /

HEDDA. Will you both stop it?

I'm old. I'm old and I'm fat.

*Beat.*

JULIE. You're not old yet dear. Plenty of time for that.

*Beat.*

GEORGE. Look! The library! /

HEDDA. George we're going to have to fire this cleaner.

*Beat.*

GEORGE. Fire Bertha?

HEDDA. Is that her name?

GEORGE. But we can't /

HEDDA. She's left her things all over the table. This ugly old hat /

GEORGE. Hedda... /

HEDDA. What's the point in a cleaner who just makes more mess?

GEORGE. Hedda that's Auntie Julie's hat.

*Beat.*

HEDDA. And a very nice hat it is too.

JULIE (*picking up the hat*). What's more, it's not old. (*Donning the hat.*) In fact, this is the first time I've worn it.

GEORGE. And doesn't it look lovely on her Hedda?

HEDDA. Very lovely /

JULIE. No need for that.

HEDDA. But now that you have it on /

JULIE. I'll be getting back to Auntie Rina then.

GEORGE. So soon?

JULIE. She shouldn't be alone for long you know /

HEDDA. Julia!

*Beat.*

It really is a very nice hat.

*Beat.*

JULIE. Poor Hedda. You do try don't you?

I'll come and visit you often now you're back. We'll have such a nice time.

*Beat.*

*Exit* GEORGE *and* JULIE.

(*Off.*) We'll be seeing you later dear.

GEORGE (*off*). I'll come round after lunch, and you'll send Auntie Rina my love in the meantime…

*Front door.*

HEDDA *breathing. Puts her hands slowly to her head.*

HEDDA (*soft*). This is killing me this is killing me this is killing me this is killing me this is killing me this is killing me this is killing me this is /

*Enter* BERTHA. *With hoover.*

HEDDA*'s hands still at her head.*

*Beat.*

BERTHA. Hi.

*Beat.*

You're Hedda right?

HEDDA. Guilty.

*Beat.*

BERTHA. Do you mind if I…?

HEDDA. Knock yourself out.

BERTHA. Thanks.

*Plugs in the hoover.*

*Hoovers.*

HEDDA *stares at her.*

BERTHA *hoovers.*

HEDDA *stares at her.*

*Eventually:*

(*Turning off the hoover.*) Can I help you?

HEDDA. With what?

BERTHA. I don't know.

HEDDA. Neither do I.

BERTHA. It's just I want to get the hoovering done. The dust in these old houses, gets everywhere.

HEDDA. Yes. It's horrible.

*Beat.*

BERTHA. That's just the way they are. But people like to do them up. That's the plan isn't it? To do it up?

HEDDA. That is the plan.

BERTHA. I'm not so keen myself, find them a bit spooky. I know it's just the wood expanding but it's like the house is talking. Do you know what I mean?

HEDDA. I know exactly what you mean. It's been talking to me all morning.

*Beat.*

BERTHA. What's it been saying?

*Beat.*

*They laugh, an edge.*

I'll take this upstairs. Nice meeting you /

HEDDA. Wait! I don't suppose you. Brought any coffee with
you? Did you?

BERTHA. Coffee?

HEDDA. Just in case you thought to pick up some groceries,
seeing as we just arrived…

BERTHA. I didn't think of that.

If you'd told the agency, they'd have told me but no one told
the agency.

*Beat.*

There's a village. Maybe a half-hour's walk…

*Exit* BERTHA.

HEDDA *and the house. The cold old ugliness of it.*

HEDDA. Fuck…

HEDDA *to the piano. Touches it, gentle.*

Hello old thing. Did you miss me?

Poor old thing…

*Presses herself into it.*

*The House.*

HEDDA *to the garden doors and opens the shutters. Light
all over her.*

*Enter* GEORGE.

*She ignores him.*

GEORGE. What are you looking at?

HEDDA. The leaves. So withered already.

I love the autumn.

*Beat.*

I hate the autumn.

GEORGE. You know, that really wasn't necessary with the hat.

HEDDA. It wasn't deliberate.

GEORGE. But you shouldn't say nasty things about hats anyway /

HEDDA. I'll make it up to her. We'll have her round for dinner and I'll do that celeriac thing she likes.

GEORGE. She'd love that.

HEDDA. Fine /

GEORGE. And there's something else you could do.

HEDDA. What.

GEORGE. She really does wish, after all this time, you'd /

HEDDA. Oh no. No no no /

GEORGE. But even Bertha was happy to call her Auntie Julie!

HEDDA. Oh, well if the Cleaner /

GEORGE. Look Hedda she's an old woman and /

HEDDA. So am I!

*Beat.*

GEORGE. You know what Hedda /

HEDDA. No George I don't know what, I really have no idea what. My piano. Is doing. In the kitchen.

GEORGE. I can explain that. You see, Auntie Julie and I thought that this might not actually be a kitchen.

*Beat.*

HEDDA. You're really going to have to give me more than that George.

GEORGE. We thought that this might actually be a Living Space.

*Beat.*

It's what people like, apparently, big spaces where the whole family can /

HEDDA. What family?

*Beat.*

GEORGE. We thought you might want to give little recitals. You used to play so well /

HEDDA. Much as it has long been an ambition of mine to give Little Recitals in a kitchen /

GEORGE. Living Space /

HEDDA. It won't work George! There's steam and moisture and the temperature fluctuates so you may as well just get it over with and take a hatchet to her right now.

*Beat.*

We'll have to get the men to move her in with The General where she belongs.

GEORGE. But Hedda they're very expensive, just to come out for that /

HEDDA. I think I'd like to put my desk here. I'd like to look out at the garden. At the trees /

*The doorbell rings.*

Oh fuck what now /

GEORGE. I'll get it.

*Exit* GEORGE.

*Again. A little too long.*

HEDDA. It's ridiculous, at this time in the morning /

*Again.*

*Front door.*

THEA *(off).* I'm sorry to burst in like this but I needed to see you.

HEDDA *stands.*

GEORGE (*off*). Thea /

THEA (*off*). I went to the flat but you weren't there /

GEORGE (*off*). Thea wait /

*Enter* THEA *and* GEORGE.

*Stop.*

Um.

*Beat.*

THEA. Auntie Rina's really sick did you know that?

GEORGE. Yes. Thea. I /

THEA. I didn't know where you were Auntie Julie had to tell me /

GEORGE. I'm sorry, we've moved, we've only just /

THEA. No one told me.

GEORGE. How could we tell you?

*Beat.*

THEA. It's fine. It's fine. I was just –

I'd imagined you there. All this time. And then you weren't…

HEDDA. Thea.

*Pause.*

GEORGE. Shall we –

Would you like to sit down?

THEA. I don't want to sit down. I want to talk.

GEORGE. Do you mind if I sit down?

THEA. I want you to listen to me I don't care if you do that standing up or sitting down.

HEDDA *laughs*.

Do you see! Do you see what she /

GEORGE. Thea /

THEA. But she's mocking me!

HEDDA. I wasn't mocking you /

THEA. She laughed at me!

HEDDA. I laughed admiringly. In admiration.

*Beat*.

THEA (*to* GEORGE). I need you to call Elijah.

HEDDA. Elijah?

GEORGE. My old student Elijah?

THEA. I need you to invite him for dinner /

HEDDA. What do you have to do with Elijah?

THEA. I'm not talking to you Hedda.

*Beat*.

(*To* GEORGE.) We wrote a book, we wrote it together /

HEDDA. How did you write a /

THEA. I can't be constantly interrupted!

Don't you see

that I can't? I need you to understand that and

I need you to invite Elijah for dinner.

GEORGE. You need us to invite Elijah for dinner?

THEA. Yes.

GEORGE. Tonight?

THEA. Yes.

GEORGE. But Elijah isn't here any more /

THEA. He's here now.

GEORGE. I don't think you understand, he's not well. The last time I saw him he /

THEA. I know. I know everything.

GEORGE. But is he /

THEA. He's sober.

GEORGE. My god…

THEA. He's been completely sober for two years now.

GEORGE. And he wrote a /

THEA. We wrote a /

GEORGE. Who published it?

THEA. It's online. Anyone can read it you just pay what you can and we didn't expect but it's been a bit of a thing /

GEORGE. What kind of a thing?

THEA. A success. Which was good at first but then he got this idea into his head. That he wanted to come back and

finish his PhD. So he's meeting with the university today but

the truth is

it's not good for him to be here. It's not good for me to be here either but I came because he came and he can't be alone /

GEORGE. I see.

THEA. I just need you to look after him tonight. And tomorrow we'll go away again. He talks about you all the time. He really loved you you know.

GEORGE. Well that's. Of course I also /

THEA. And you owe him a duty of care. Because you failed once before.

*Pause.*

HEDDA. Well I think this is all very clear.

GEORGE. Is it?

HEDDA. Do what Thea says and invite Elijah round /

GEORGE. You're sure?

HEDDA. Tell him we'll pay for a cab if he needs it.

GEORGE. Right. Good. Do you have his /

THEA. Yes!

*Gives* GEORGE *her phone.*

HEDDA. And be very nice. You remember how sensitive he could /

THEA. Dad!

*Beat.*

His number's there but don't use my phone.

GEORGE. Okay.

THEA. And if he asks tell him you heard at the university, and you got his number from the department?

GEORGE. Okay.

THEA. Okay.

GEORGE. Okay.

*Beat.*

It's so good to see you.

*Exit* GEORGE.

HEDDA *and* THEA *and The General.*

*Beat.*

HEDDA. I'd offer you some coffee but there isn't /

THEA. What are you doing here?

HEDDA. What am *I* doing /

THEA. In this house?

*Beat.*

HEDDA. You know, I really don't know. Some mad idea of
    your father's /

THEA. Why is it so big?

Like it's swallowed us.

*Pause.*

HEDDA. How are you?

THEA. Why?

HEDDA. Just making conversation.

THEA. Why?

HEDDA. Habit. I guess.

THEA. I don't want to 'make conversation' with you.
    Everything you touch dies. You're toxic.

HEDDA. Thea just /

THEA. Hedda just what?

HEDDA. I wish you wouldn't call me that /

THEA. It's your name.

HEDDA. Well George is your father's name and you don't call
    him George.

You used to call me Mummy.

THEA. Because you were my mother /

HEDDA. I Am your /

THEA. And I was frightened of you /

HEDDA. Please don't /

THEA. You used to pull

my

hair.

*Beat.*

You said you were going to burn it off /

HEDDA. I never /

THEA. Stop lying!

*Beat.*

I can't talk to you if you won't stop lying. My therapist said /

HEDDA. Your therapist was a fucking quack who did more damage to this family /

THEA *goes.*

And what does your husband think about you running down here after Elijah?

THEA *stops.*

THEA. Everything he thinks is irrelevant.

HEDDA. Much as I sympathise with that position /

THEA. Everything he thinks is irrelevant because I've left him.

HEDDA. What do you mean 'left him'?

THEA. I got up in the morning and I packed his son's lunchbox and I took him to school and then I got on a train and I'll never go back.

*Beat.*

HEDDA. That's absurd.

THEA. It's the opposite of absurd /

HEDDA. I wasn't happy about you dropping out of university /

THEA. It's logical /

HEDDA. Shacking up with some boring man nearly twice your age /

THEA. Reasonable, serious /

HEDDA. But you've made your choices and it's important to /

THEA. It's not important /

HEDDA. Marriage Is important /

THEA. It's just a habit. Like conversation.

People are alone. So they get married. And then they have conversations. And they think they're not alone any more but they are.

*Beat.*

HEDDA. Was he. Unkind to you?

THEA. No.

HEDDA. He didn't /

THEA. Nothing like that. We just didn't have anything to say to each other /

HEDDA. But you can't live like this! Running around making these whimsical decisions, no focus no commitment no –

It's a failure of living.

THEA. To stay with him and have babies would be a failure of living but then again you already know that.

Don't you.

*Pause.*

HEDDA. You've really left him?

*Beat.*

How extraordinary.

THEA. It's not extraordinary. It's just what you have to do to live properly.

HEDDA. And what exactly is 'living properly'?

THEA. There are real relationships two people can have. Where you understand each other.

HEDDA. Oh, well of course if you can have babies with someone who 'understands' you then /

THEA. You have such a limited way of thinking. It's not like that with Elijah. We're not lovers. We're

collaborators.

HEDDA. 'Collaborators.'

THEA. We work together. We write together. We're equals.

HEDDA. 'Equals.'

THEA. And there's no equality in love.

HEDDA (*smiles*). Is that what he says?

THEA. We know how to speak to each other. We tell each other everything.

HEDDA. So he knows you're here?

*Beat.*

THEA. He will. We trust each other completely. Even though I'm so stupid /

HEDDA. You're not stupid /

THEA. No I really am. That's why I made the choices I made. But it's getting better, my thoughts are getting clearer I feel like I'm

surfacing. From deep water.

*The House.*

HEDDA. But what are you going to do now?

THEA. I just have to be where Elijah is and he has to be where I am and we have to do the work.

HEDDA. When we last saw him he could barely hold a pen, let alone write a book.

THEA. He's different now.

HEDDA. How?

THEA. It happened slowly. It was like I had some kind of power over him.

HEDDA. Power?

THEA. He just stopped drinking. I never told him to or asked him to but the more time we spent together the more he realised it's possible to start again.

HEDDA. So you saved him did you?

THEA. I think you can only save yourself. In the end.

HEDDA. Oh come on Thea, you're really trying to tell me you haven't enjoyed the influence you've had?

THEA. You don't understand. It's so hard to do what he's done and it's so easy to undo it just one drink would /

HEDDA. You should have more faith in him.

THEA. I do! But it's. Being back here it –

And that's Elijah's problem. He can't let go of the past and you have to let go of the past to be free.

GEORGE *coming back.*

HEDDA. Thea I think we should keep all this between us. Your father's not exactly

discreet. And you wouldn't want this getting back to Elijah would you?

THEA. No! No he /

HEDDA. Good. It'll be our secret.

*Enter* GEORGE.

GEORGE. Well that went very well!

THEA. He'll come?

GEORGE. He will.

THEA. Thank god!

GEORGE. I'm really looking forward to hearing all about this book /

*Enter* BERTHA.

BERTHA. Sorry to interrupt but /

HEDDA. Just a minute please /

BERTHA. Yeah but /

HEDDA. Can't you see we're talking to our daughter?

BERTHA. Yeah but there's a man in the garden.

*Beat.*

HEDDA *to garden door.*

HEDDA. It's Brack.

*Opens the door. Waves.*

BRACK (*off*). Hedda! You know I can walk right up through
    the –

*Enter* BRACK.

*Sees* THEA. *Stops.*

Thea!

What a lovely /

THEA. I was just going. Bye Dad. And thanks.

GEORGE. No need to thank me.

HEDDA. I'll just walk Thea out /

THEA. I don't need walking out I'm not a dog.

HEDDA. Stop being so sensitive Thea I /

*Exit* THEA.

Excuse me.

*Exit* HEDDA.

(*Off.*) And will someone get me some coffee before I kill
myself?

*Front door.*

*Beat.*

BERTHA. That was your daughter?

GEORGE. Thea, yes.

BERTHA. Should I make up a spare room?

GEORGE. Yes. No! I don't know. Ask Hedda.

BERTHA. Okay /

GEORGE. No don't ask Hedda!

*Beat.*

Maybe try not to think about it. That's the best thing.

BERTHA. Okay.

GEORGE. Thanks Bertha.

*Exit* BERTHA.

BRACK. So! Welcome back! How are you?

GEORGE. A little jetlagged, but happy to be home.

BRACK. Speaking of home, are you pleased?

*The open-arm gesture.*

GEORGE. Very!

BRACK. And Hedda?

GEORGE. Thrilled.

BRACK. Can't have Hedda anything less than thrilled.

GEORGE. It'd be the end of us.

*They laugh. They too have often laughed about Hedda over the years.*

BRACK. God, do you remember –

*Laughs.*

It came back to me, coming over the field. Do you remember the thing with the horse?

GEORGE. The horse?

BRACK. You must remember! You'd come for dinner and we somehow stayed up all night /

GEORGE. Oh god the horse!

BRACK. We were so drunk and we went for a walk /

GEORGE. With the terrible wine!

BRACK. You brought that wine…

GEORGE. And there was this field of unbroken horses and Hedda just /

BRACK. Climbed up onto a horse!

GEORGE. It was your fault! I remember now! You gave her a leg-up!

BRACK. I wanted to see what would happen.

GEORGE. Do you remember how it bucked? I feel sick thinking about it…

BRACK. You were shouting 'Get off the horse Hedda! Get off the horse Hedda!' As though she could!

GEORGE. It's not like she ever listened to me anyway /

BRACK. And it just tore off /

GEORGE. And she fell…

The sun was up. I thought she'd broken her neck.

Running across the field and Hedda immobile

on the grass.

*Beat.*

BRACK. Then we rolled her over and she was just /

GEORGE. Laughing /

BRACK. Laughing and laughing /

GEORGE. That's right /

BRACK. Her legs wouldn't stop shaking /

GEORGE. Shock to the system /

BRACK. I carried her all the way back. All the way in my arms and she wouldn't stop laughing…

*Pause.*

GEORGE. Must have been twenty years ago now...

BRACK. How did the time pass?

*They think about it.*

GEORGE. God I'm sorry, I haven't offered you anything but the truth is we don't really have anything yet.

BRACK. I wasn't going to stay. I just wanted to come and say hello, check you were settling in.

GEORGE. We've quite a bit to do before we're completely settled.

BRACK. Oh yes?

GEORGE. The house itself needs work, then there's new furniture to buy. But Hedda will take care of that.

BRACK. She's good at that sort of thing.

GEORGE. I'll be busy with the professorship anyway.

BRACK. About that, I was having dinner with the Vice Chancellor last night.

GEORGE. How is he?

BRACK. Excited.

GEORGE. About the professorship?

BRACK. Of course. But he also mentioned your old student Elijah is back in town.

GEORGE. Yes I know that. Thea told us.

*Beat.*

BRACK. How did Thea know?

GEORGE. They're friends.

BRACK. Friends?

GEORGE. And she says he's completely well again, I mean completely sober.

BRACK. I heard that too.

GEORGE. And that he's written a book. Apparently it's been a huge success.

BRACK. There's talk of a permanent position if he finishes his PhD.

GEORGE. I'll do everything I can to help him. He was so brilliant and it was awful when he had to drop out.

BRACK. Just awful.

GEORGE. I feel responsible, I was his supervisor after all. But I am a bit worried /

BRACK. About what?

GEORGE. We can try and secure the necessary funding, but it's so much harder these days. What is he going to live on?

*Enter* HEDDA.

HEDDA. George is forever worrying about what people are going to live on. It's very boring.

GEORGE. We're talking about Elijah.

HEDDA. What about Elijah?

GEORGE. You know there's no help for him from home.

BRACK. There isn't?

GEORGE. God no. He was on every bursary under the sun, and a scholarship for the MA.

BRACK. There are the book proceeds.

HEDDA. No there aren't. It's all nice and friendly pay-what-you-want sort of thing.

GEORGE. I'll talk it all through with him over dinner tonight.

BRACK. Tonight? But you're coming to my party tonight!

HEDDA. Did you forget my love?

GEORGE. Shit… It's just this morning. Everything's so /

BRACK. I wouldn't worry, I'd be surprised if he actually came.

GEORGE. But he said he would. Just now on the phone.

BRACK. You're sure?

*Beat.*

HEDDA. What are you getting at Brack.

BRACK. Think about it George.

HEDDA. He is thinking. That's his thinking face.

BRACK. Your last book, the one that brought you all your recent success.

GEORGE. Yes?

BRACK. I seem to remember you told me that the central thesis was Elijah's.

GEORGE. Yes?

*Beat.*

But Brack! You said at the time, when I asked you for your opinion, specifically your legal opinion, you said it was perfectly natural /

BRACK. Did I?

GEORGE. Yes! A supervisor and student working in the same area, you said of course ideas would be shared /

BRACK. Up to a point.

GEORGE. 'Up to a'? /

BRACK. And I suppose we didn't expect him to come back. Considering the

state he was in.

*Beat.*

GEORGE. But I didn't

plagiarise did I?

BRACK. I'm sorry I didn't catch that.

GEORGE. I said it wasn't / pla–

BRACK. I just can't hear. That word. That you are using.

*Beat.*

GEORGE. What am I going to do?

BRACK. We'll have to find out what his intentions are.

GEORGE. Intentions?

BRACK. It might get difficult with your new position.

GEORGE. The professorship?

BRACK. You can't expect to take up the post if he launches an inquiry.

GEORGE. Elijah would never! I looked after him, we both did /

HEDDA. Leave me out of it.

GEORGE. Brack this is impossible. We've taken out a mortgage, I need the salary, and the commission for the book /

BRACK. Then you might want to hold off on any unnecessary expenses for the time being.

*Gazes, mild, around the kitchen.*

Hedda.

HEDDA. I don't see what this has to do with me.

BRACK. Don't you? How nice. (*To* GEORGE.) I'll be back around six for a drink then, and we'll head into town together.

GEORGE. Right.

BRACK. No need to show me out, Hedda, I feel completely at home here already.

*Exit* BRACK, *garden.*

*Silence.*

GEORGE. What are you thinking about?

Hedda?

*Beat.*

Hedda?

HEDDA. Just how long someone can expect to survive trapped in this ghastly wallpaper.

*Beat.*

Well it won't be that long if it all goes tits-up and we lose the house.

GEORGE. We won't. We'll just have to be careful.
Unnecessary expenses, like Brack said /

HEDDA. Such as the cleaner?

*Beat.*

GEORGE. Poor Bertha. She's so nice.

HEDDA. And my car?

GEORGE. We certainly can't afford more than one car! I wonder whether there's a bus into town for you...

*Pause.*

Auntie Julie will have to pick you up...

HEDDA. Julia pick me up?

GEORGE. She said this morning, she wanted to go on some little trips with you /

HEDDA. Little Trips?

GEORGE. And now the house won't be keeping you busy it'll be nice for you to /

HEDDA. What do you mean Little Trips?

GEORGE. You know, to galleries and museums /

HEDDA. Oh god.

GEORGE. National Trust houses /

HEDDA. Oh God!

GEORGE. You know Hedda sometimes you can be very
  overdramatic.

  *Pause.*

HEDDA. I see

  how it's going to be.

  *Stands.*

  Well at least I still have one thing left to play with.

GEORGE. Your piano?

HEDDA. No George. Not my piano. My guns. General Gabler's
  guns.

  *Exit* HEDDA.

GEORGE. I told you I don't like you messing around with
  those things. It's not safe Hedda, it really isn't safe!

  *End of Act One.*

## ACT TWO

*Shutters and doors wide to the day. Late-afternoon light.*

*Piano replaced by* HEDDA*'s desk. On the desk, the gun case, open.*

HEDDA, *dressed, by the garden door loading a gun.*

*Looks up, sudden.*

HEDDA. Hello Brack!

BRACK (*off, far*). Hedda! Hello!

HEDDA. I'm going to shoot you Brack.

*Raises the gun.*

BRACK (*off, nearer*). Don't point that at me it /

*Gunshot.*

(*Off.*) Jesus Christ!

HEDDA. Oops. I didn't hit you did I?

*Raises it again.*

BRACK (*off, near*). Put it down it's not funny!

HEDDA *laughs. Lowers the gun.*

*Enter* BRACK.

What the hell do you think you're doing?

HEDDA. Me? Nothing. Just

shooting at the sky.

BRACK. Where did you get this?

*Takes the gun.*

HEDDA. It was The General's.

BRACK. Beautiful…

HEDDA. I think so.

BRACK. Licensed of course?

HEDDA. Of course.

*Beat.*

BRACK. Let's put this away now.

*Puts the gun in its case.*

HEDDA. Oh come on Brack. What else am I supposed to do, stuck out here in the middle of nowhere?

BRACK. Cheer up. I've got you a present.

*A packet of coffee.*

HEDDA. Coffee!

BRACK. Your wish is my command /

HEDDA. You're so sweet. But I'm already counting down till I can have a real drink.

BRACK. A healthy way to spend your afternoon.

HEDDA. I am healthy! These days. Some arbitrary idea of George's, six o'clock in the evening being acceptable gin time, five fifty-nine not /

BRACK. So for the time being…?

*The coffee.*

HEDDA. I can't. I'll never sleep.

BRACK. I'm always just too late where you're concerned…

HEDDA *laughs, reaches for the coffee. He snaps it away.*

Not that you deserve it. Trying to murder me like that.

HEDDA. Don't! I'll have it for breakfast tomorrow and think of you.

*He gives it to her.*

Thank you. Now sit the fuck down and talk to me before I die of boredom.

BRACK. George not around to entertain you?

HEDDA. He went scurrying off to his aunts as soon as he could get away.

BRACK. I'd have come earlier, had I known.

HEDDA. Then you'd have sat here all by yourself.

BRACK. Why's that?

HEDDA. I was having a nap.

BRACK. Alone?

HEDDA. All alone.

BRACK. Pity.

HEDDA. I'm used to it.

BRACK. Why don't you have some friends round, you know, like a normal person.

HEDDA. What friends? You're my only friend.

BRACK. I missed you too.

HEDDA. Then you could have come to visit.

BRACK. I don't remember being invited.

HEDDA. Never stopped you before…

BRACK. Anyway, you had enough fun without me.

HEDDA. Fun. Good one.

*Beat.*

BRACK. George seems to think you had a great time.

HEDDA. Well he did! Pottering around libraries and archives, everyone treating him like some kind of a genius. I swear if I hear the words Domestic or Brabant one more time…

BRACK. His work has always been his passion.

HEDDA. And I respect his passion. We've just always had different areas of interest.

BRACK. I can see that...

HEDDA. But as for me, there was no one to talk to. No one who wanted to talk to me...

BRACK. Their loss.

HEDDA. You know, it's recently come to my attention that I don't actually exist. I mean I'm not a real person. Just

clever Dr Tesman's nice wife who cooks very well and looks very well and –

*Beat.*

You wake up

one day and you've attached yourself to one person. And by attaching yourself to one person you've attached yourself to an entire life and you don't know how you

sleptwalked into your present. And your future became your past.

BRACK. But with someone you love /

HEDDA. Don't be sentimental, it doesn't suit you.

BRACK. Sentimental?

HEDDA. My husband is an academic.

BRACK. Yes.

HEDDA. Academics are boring.

BRACK. Strange to hear from someone who was one herself.

HEDDA. There's nothing like growing old for curing you of your naive ideas about things...

BRACK. Then why did you?

HEDDA. Why did I what?

BRACK. Marry him.

*Beat.*

HEDDA. I suppose I was lonely.

BRACK. Lonely?

HEDDA. My father had just died and. He was very ill for a long time. And then he was very ill in hospital for a long time. And just when I'd assumed he wasn't actually capable of it, dying, he

did.

*Beat.*

I remember he looked rather pleased with himself…

BRACK *laughs. They laugh.*

Anyway it doesn't matter. George is a good man.

BRACK. A very good man.

HEDDA. And he's good at what he does. I mean, he doesn't have

flair. But he works hard, he's diligent.

BRACK. So you knew he'd be really successful one day?

HEDDA. What? No. I was more concerned with being really successful myself.

But then we got pregnant.

*Beat.*

It's more that he was just

there. We were friends and he was kind and he loved me. He made it very clear that he loved me so in the end I made a choice. What's wrong with that?

BRACK. Nothing. I've never had anything but profound respect for the institution of marriage. In theory.

HEDDA. But not in practice?

BRACK. I've always felt I can leave that up to others to enjoy.

HEDDA. How thoughtful of you.

BRACK. For myself I've always preferred less

conventional arrangements.

HEDDA. And for myself I wasn't paying attention and I got on the wrong train.

BRACK. Then why don't you jump off. Stretch your

legs.

HEDDA. I'll never jump off.

BRACK. Why?

HEDDA. There might be someone waiting /

BRACK. To catch you when you fall?

*Beat.*

HEDDA. I don't want that and I never have.

I'd rather just

stay in the carriage with my one other person, watching the world going through my reflection...

BRACK. But what if, hypothetically, someone wanted to join you and your one other person in the carriage?

HEDDA. Someone fun you could really talk to about all sorts of interesting things?

BRACK. Nothing academic about him /

HEDDA. Someone who'd leave you to your own reflection when you wanted?

*Beat.*

BRACK. Purely hypothetically...

*Front door. Whistling.*

Right on time, your one other person.

HEDDA (*soft*). And the train goes on…

*Enter* GEORGE. *Shopping, lots.*

GEORGE. Brack! Sorry I was out.

BRACK. Hedda's been keeping me entertained.

GEORGE. Good. I've picked up the car.

BRACK. How is it?

GEORGE. It's a car.

HEDDA. George. What is all that?

GEORGE. Books! Lots of wonderful books.

HEDDA. I thought we were supposed to be being careful?

GEORGE. Not with books, I need books.

HEDDA. Of course you do. How silly of me.

GEORGE. And look what I picked up…

*A printout.*

It's Elijah's, the one everyone's talking about. I had to print it off, quite annoying really but of course I appreciate this accessibility gesture of his.

HEDDA. You've looked at it?

GEORGE. Yes.

HEDDA. And?

GEORGE. It's excellent.

HEDDA. So what's new?

GEORGE. But he's improved. He could be a little wild, too caught up in his own ideas. With this there's a focus he didn't quite have before… By the way, this is a celeriac isn't it?

*A celeriac.*

HEDDA. That is a celeriac.

GEORGE (*pleased*). It doesn't look at all like celery…

HEDDA. Looks can be deceptive.

GEORGE. Anyway, I'd like to finish off this chapter before we go if that's alright?

BRACK. As long as we're at the restaurant for seven.

GEORGE. And since we're on the subject, Hedda, Auntie Julie won't be joining you for dinner.

*Beat.*

HEDDA. Was Julia joining me for dinner?

GEORGE. You said to invite her. Because of the hat.

HEDDA. Oh. The hat.

GEORGE. But Auntie Rina's really not well /

HEDDA. Isn't she always really not /

GEORGE. She's worse.

*Beat.*

HEDDA. Then of course Julia should stay with her.

GEORGE. But she wanted me to pass on, she thought you were looking so well. That the new weight really suits you.

HEDDA. The what?

GEORGE. She said they always thought you were too thin /

HEDDA. These perpetual aunts!

GEORGE. I never thought so myself, but they do know about these things…

*Exit* GEORGE *with printout.*

*Beat.*

HEDDA. Bitch.

*They laugh.*

BRACK. What's all this about a hat?

HEDDA. God I'm being haunted by this hat! It's nothing. It was so stupid. She'd bought a hat, the sort of idiotic thing she does to try and impress me, and.

I pretended I thought it was the cleaner's and I called it an ugly old hat.

BRACK. Hedda! How could you do such a thing to that sweet old lady?

HEDDA. Believe me, after thirty years of her you begin to have really violent thoughts...

*Beat.*

Sometimes I want to do something hurtful. It comes over me. Like a sickness.

And then I do it.

And then I feel terrible, really terrible...

And then I suppose I feel nothing at all.

BRACK. You know what your problem is?

HEDDA. Tell me what my problem is Brack.

BRACK. You're not happy.

HEDDA. Why should I be happy?

BRACK. For a start you've got the house you've always wanted.

HEDDA. Oh Brack. Even you?

*Beat.*

BRACK. But George said, when it finally came on the market, he said this house –

It's not true is it?

BRACK *laughs.*

HEDDA. I'm glad you have a sense of humour. You need one where George and I are concerned.

BRACK. But where on earth did he get the idea from?

HEDDA. I can't. It's too ridiculous /

BRACK. Please.

HEDDA. To be fair to him there is some truth in it. It was after Thea was born, I went sort of

numb. Couldn't read. Couldn't think. Couldn't write or –

*Beat.*

George used to make me go on these endless walks to get me out of the house and he'd talk about. Anything else. Because we couldn't talk about. That. Never have, thank god...

But he was desperate for me to be happy and I was desperate listening to him, and one afternoon we could see this house from a hill. It looked so pretty in the twilight. And just for something to say, anything at all to save him from my silence I said 'One day I want to live there.'

BRACK. That was it?

HEDDA. Little did I know that he clung to this idea for thirty. Years.

BRACK. He does have a certain tenacity...

HEDDA. So here we are! All our money sunk into this horrible house. An old woman's house. An old woman who took thirty years to die and finally died.

Can't you smell it?

Like

flowers the day after a wedding.

*The House.*

BRACK. That is the saddest thing I've ever heard.

*They look at each other.*

*They laugh.*

HEDDA. Well I've made my bed and here I am lying in it and it's just. Fine.

*Beat.*

But sometimes I think I'm feverish, all tangled up in the sheets /

BRACK. You know what you need /

HEDDA. Tell me what I need Brack.

BRACK. You need something to do. Something serious that engages you /

HEDDA. Oh certainly. There are all sorts of serious things just waiting to be engaged with by middle-aged women with no qualifications.

BRACK. I wouldn't describe you as unqualified.

HEDDA. An aborted career as a historian and a neglected talent for the piano? Yes, I'm fending off the headhunters.

BRACK. Don't be sarcastic with me.

HEDDA. I also know how to use a breast pump. Do you know how to use a breast pump?

BRACK. I can't say I do.

HEDDA. Amazing you're the judge and I'm not.

BRACK. Why don't you start teaching again?

HEDDA. Is that Really your best suggestion?

BRACK. I thought you liked teaching piano!

HEDDA. I had to do it or I'd have gone completely insane. But as for something that's actually engaging...

*Beat.*

It must be nice being you. Sitting there in judgement on people, their lives in your hands. What does that actually feel like?

BRACK. What?

HEDDA. Power?

*Beat.*

BRACK. That is an extremely perverted impression of what I do, unbefitting the solemnity of my office.

HEDDA. Is that what they tell you to say?

BRACK. Besides, there's lots of excitement ahead for you both.

HEDDA. You mean the professorship?

BRACK. For one.

HEDDA. Well if it were my professorship then perhaps I'd have something to be proud of. But all that became George's Thing a long time ago...

No, there's only one thing I'm good at now.

BRACK. Which is?

HEDDA. Boring myself to death! And here comes The Professor, dressed for a night on the town...

*Enter* GEORGE. *Exactly the same clothes but with a bow tie.*

GEORGE. How are we doing?

HEDDA. I want a gin.

*Goes and makes gin and tonics.*

GEORGE. It's not quite six yet...

HEDDA. You see how he treats me?

BRACK. When we're gone you can drink yourself sick.

HEDDA. Your little lads' night out. Pathetic really...

BRACK. Don't be jealous.

HEDDA. I'm not jealous. I'll have Elijah to keep me company.

*Beat.*

BRACK. He'll stay after we're gone?

HEDDA. I don't see why not.

BRACK. But are you sure that that's entirely…

GEORGE. You remember how he could be? He really could be quite /

HEDDA. According to Thea he's a saint these days. Or is it Thea who's the saint? I forget…

BRACK. But to be alone with /

HEDDA. Thea's coming too.

GEORGE. She is?

HEDDA. I persuaded her this morning. Didn't take much persuading, the poor girl's obsessed /

*Doorbell.*

GEORGE. That'll be him.

*Pause.*

HEDDA. Well let him in.

GEORGE. I'm feeling a little nervous.

HEDDA. Well he might be about to ruin your career.

GEORGE. Thank you for taking this so seriously Hedda.

BRACK. I wonder whether we should have a strategy, for approaching the situation sensitively /

GEORGE. I think we should just behave normally.

HEDDA. When have you ever behaved normally?

GEORGE. Exactly like that. I'll suggest something perfectly sensible and my wife can ridicule me.

*A man at the garden door.*

BRACK. Ahh George, come on now…

GEORGE. No I'm serious! This is upsetting for me /

*Enter the man,* ELIJAH. *They don't see him.*

*He sort of stands there.*

HEDDA. Well it isn't exactly normal not to answer the door is it.

GEORGE. I hope you aren't getting into one of your moods…

*Turns.*

*Sees* ELIJAH. *Stops.*

ELIJAH. Hello Dr Tesman.

GEORGE. Elijah!

ELIJAH. I rang the bell but /

GEORGE. I'm so sorry! We just had a little thing, a. Never
   mind come in, well you are in /

HEDDA. You're babbling George.

GEORGE. You remember Hedda?

ELIJAH. Thank you for inviting me for dinner Mrs Tesman.

HEDDA. Mrs Tesman is it?

*They laugh.*

ELIJAH. What?

HEDDA. We won't have any of that, I feel old enough without
   That.

GEORGE. And our friend Brack, I don't know if you two
   ever…

*Beat.*

ELIJAH. You're the judge.

BRACK. Well remembered.

ELIJAH. I haven't forgotten everything.

   Just some things.

   *Awkward beat.*

   This

   is a new house.

GEORGE. It is!

ELIJAH. I'll miss your flat. It was like home to me.

GEORGE. Well there's no reason this /

HEDDA. Gin for all! Elijah?

*A glass.*

ELIJAH. No thanks.

HEDDA. Oh of course. Brack?

BRACK. Gin for all except Elijah! To your new home, and many happy years ahead.

*They drink.*

ELIJAH *waits.*

GEORGE. So Elijah, I hear you want to take up your PhD again?

ELIJAH. Yes.

GEORGE. That's excellent. I'll do what I can to /

ELIJAH. I don't need help.

*Awkward beat.*

GEORGE. Well we'll see. But look what I picked up today…

*The printout.*

ELIJAH. What is it?

GEORGE. Your book! I haven't finished it yet /

ELIJAH. Don't bother. It's not interesting…

BRACK. But it's been so well received?

ELIJAH. I needed it to be well received so I wrote it to be well received.

BRACK. Very sensible.

ELIJAH. If I'm going to start over I had to get their attention. That's all it was.

GEORGE. Well I think it's extremely interesting.

ELIJAH. When this comes out though –

*A book, in manuscript.*

This one I put myself into.

GEORGE. What's the subject?

ELIJAH. A continuation.

GEORGE. Of what?

ELIJAH. The book.

GEORGE. Which book?

ELIJAH. This book.

GEORGE. That book!

ELIJAH. That book.

GEORGE. But you can't continue it. This is…

*A Short History of History: Past and Present.*

ELIJAH. And this is *A Short History of History: The Future.*

*Beat.*

GEORGE. But we don't know anything about the future.

ELIJAH. There are still things to say about it.

*Gives* GEORGE *the book.*

*Pause.*

GEORGE. Well your handwriting's certainly improved.

BRACK. You haven't been influenced by George's Luddite prejudices have you?

GEORGE (*reading, half there*). It was to slow him down. He thinks too fast, gets carried away…

ELIJAH. It was a good suggestion.

GEORGE. Though I will admit to being a bit sneaky. Having you type it up afterwards was the only way I could get you to edit.

*Beat.*

ELIJAH. Oh!

*He laughs. A potential past opens in his face.*

HEDDA. Quite the Machiavellian operator George.

GEORGE. But this isn't your handwriting?

ELIJAH. I dictated some of it.

*He raises his hand. It trembles.*

*A leaf.*

It does that. Sometimes.

*Pause.*

GEORGE. Elijah I'm /

ELIJAH. It's fine. It's done. *This* is the future. Look George, it's in two parts. The first isolates the socio-cultural forces that will operate on the future. The second explores potential paths the future could take, excavating their roots in the present and the past.

*Beat.*

GEORGE. It would never occur to me to write about that.

HEDDA. No...

GEORGE. Hang on! Didn't you propose something similar for your PhD?

HEDDA. I'm sure I didn't /

GEORGE. Yes! Not exactly the same, it was a thesis on the collapse of the nuclear family unit.

BRACK. Very Second Wave.

GEORGE. What was it your supervisor said?

HEDDA. I don't remember. He was totally immemorable /

GEORGE. That was it! 'We are not in the business of writing fairytales, Miss Gah-Blah.'

   BRACK *and* GEORGE *laugh.*

HEDDA. Do we have anything for Elijah to drink?

ELIJAH. What I wanted was for you to look at this with me.

GEORGE. Tonight?

ELIJAH. It's just the first draft, I'd be grateful for /

BRACK. But unfortunately George is coming to my party tonight.

GEORGE. I'm sorry Elijah /

BRACK. You'd be welcome to join us?

ELIJAH. I don't think so.

BRACK. You could bring the book with you.

GEORGE. We could have a reading!

BRACK. Several senior members of the university will be there. I'm sure you'd love to speak to them about /

ELIJAH. I'm sure I would. But I can't.

HEDDA. Leave him alone you two. He'd much rather have dinner with me than sit about entertaining a bunch of ageing libertines.

ELIJAH. With you?

HEDDA. And Thea.

ELIJAH. Thea's here?

   *Beat.*

HEDDA. So you have to stay. She'd be so bored, with just me for company.

   *Beat.*

ELIJAH. I'll stay.

HEDDA. Lovely.

GEORGE. You know what Elijah?

    ELIJAH *looking at* HEDDA *who is looking at him.*

ELIJAH. What?

GEORGE. I heard at the department that you might be giving a series of open lectures next year?

ELIJAH. Yes.

GEORGE. Which is a nice coincidence because I, too, am hoping to give a series of lectures on Domestic Crafts in the Medieval Brabant.

ELIJAH. Really.

GEORGE. And all this stuff about the future, is that what you're going to be lecturing on?

ELIJAH. I was thinking of bringing in some of the work from my old PhD too.

GEORGE. You were?

ELIJAH. I hope that's not awkward for you?

GEORGE. No! No no, I think it's a great /

HEDDA. George will be able to help you. He's so familiar with your PhD.

GEORGE. Yes thank you Hedda, I would of course be very happy, if you wanted I mean, to /

ELIJAH. Don't –

    *Beat.*

GEORGE. Sorry?

ELIJAH. You think I'm going to accuse you of plagiarism.

GEORGE. But Elijah I /

ELIJAH. I don't remember things. Towards the end. But I remember you were kind to me. You always supported me against the university, even when things were

bad. I've only come back to finish my PhD, get a lectureship and

take it from there.

GEORGE. You're not going to /

ELIJAH. No. I'm only going to destroy you by being vastly superior to you.

GEORGE. Well that's alright, I'd be very happy about that.

HEDDA. Does this mean I can replace the wallpaper?

GEORGE. I don't see why not.

HEDDA. Right!

*Knocks back her gin.*

Why don't you all go in there where it's comfortable and make some more drinks.

*Exit GEORGE, with gin things.*

You too Elijah.

ELIJAH. No thanks.

BRACK. But gin and tonics are practically fruit juice.

*Holds up a lemon.*

ELIJAH. Not for everyone.

BRACK. Youth of today, no fun at all...

HEDDA. Go away and make me a drink. Elijah can keep me company in here.

BRACK *stops.*

Off you pop.

*Exit BRACK.*

GEORGE *and* BRACK *together in the sitting room. They stand beneath The General and make the drinks.*

Now let's see. What can we do to entertain ourselves until Thea gets here…

*Beat.*

I know! I'll show you some very nice photos of mine and George's time in America. Wouldn't you like to see some very nice photos of mine and George's time in America?

*Gets the photo album and sits.*

The perpetual aunts made this. Isn't it nice?

*Beat.*

*Then* ELIJAH *sits next to her and looks at her all the time.*

This is mine and George's Nice Little House. You can see how the aunts have written beneath it, 'George and Hedda's Little' /

ELIJAH. Hedda

Gabler.

*Beat.*

HEDDA. Don't call me that.

ELIJAH. Why?

HEDDA. I don't like it.

ELIJAH. Why?

HEDDA. It's not my name.

ELIJAH. You didn't mind before /

HEDDA. It's different now.

ELIJAH. Hedda. Gah– /

HEDDA. Stop it /

ELIJAH. What are you Doing here? After everything you /

*Enter* GEORGE.

HEDDA. And here's a picture of George with a very interesting man. Who is he George? He was so interesting.

GEORGE. That's the Chancellor Hedda!

HEDDA. Such a memorable man.

GEORGE. We were wondering if you wanted any nibbles with your drinks?

HEDDA. We don't want any 'nibbles'. But we'll have some nuts or crisps if there are any.

*Exit* GEORGE.

ELIJAH. You said you were going to leave him, you said /

HEDDA. No I did not. What I said was that it is possible for some people /

ELIJAH. But not you?

HEDDA. Oh calm down.

ELIJAH. I'm sorry. I'm insulting your great love for Dr Tesman.

HEDDA. Why does everyone keep banging on at me about love? It's offensive.

ELIJAH. Who's been banging on at you /

HEDDA. And here is a very interesting photograph of a very interesting and rare book George found in the archives.

*Enter* GEORGE *with tray: nuts, drinks*.

GEORGE. Here we are!

HEDDA. You've brought two glasses. Elijah doesn't drink.

GEORGE. Thea's coming.

HEDDA. Oh yes.

GEORGE. You're sure you won't join us in the sitting room?

HEDDA. I need to get started on the dinner.

ELIJAH. I'll help.

GEORGE. Well just let me know if you want anything.

*Exit* GEORGE.

ELIJAH. I need you to /

HEDDA. You and your needs. Pass me the celeriac.

ELIJAH. The. What? No. I need you to tell me that with us it wasn't /

HEDDA. What?

ELIJAH. Wasn't /

HEDDA. You Need

to be careful.

And you need to pass me that celeriac.

*Beat.*

*Passes her the celeriac. She peels it.*

The way I remember it, between 'us', as you put it, is that we were equals.

ELIJAH. Yes.

HEDDA. And there's no equality in love.

ELIJAH. That's what you said /

HEDDA. Slice up that apple would you?

*Beat.*

Are you going to help me or not?

*Offers him a small kitchen knife.*

*Beat.*

*He takes it. Slices up the apple.*

There is nothing equal in love, at least as we experience it in the societies that we –

Finer slices please. Had I written the PhD I'd wanted to you could have just read that but as it is /

ELIJAH. As it is /

HEDDA. Whereas we understood each other.

ELIJAH. Yes.

*They stop chopping.*

HEDDA. And that. Is a relationship worth having.

*She chops again.*

There was something beautiful about it I thought…

ELIJAH. Beautiful?

HEDDA. This secret friendship no one else knew about /

ELIJAH. I remember /

HEDDA. You'd come round when George was teaching /

ELIJAH. And we'd talk /

HEDDA. For hours. What you were reading, what you were working on /

ELIJAH. And we'd drink /

HEDDA. All day! (*Laughs.*) The things we came up with /

ELIJAH. You recommended material to me, stuff I'd never heard of /

HEDDA. And you'd turn up the next day having read it all, ready to continue where we left off /

ELIJAH. It was like you had some power over me to make me come back, make me keep talking /

HEDDA. You think so?

ELIJAH. How did you do it?

HEDDA. It was brilliant /

ELIJAH. Why did you do it?

HEDDA. You were brilliant…

ELIJAH. But it wasn't love.

HEDDA. No. Never that.

ELIJAH. Then why?

*Pause.*

*He slices the apple. She chops the celeriac.*

HEDDA. I suppose. For the first time in years, and the last time. I felt alive.

ELIJAH. That was it?

HEDDA. That was it.

ELIJAH. Sad.

HEDDA. Sad?

Yes. I suppose I am.

Sad.

*They chop.*

But for what it's worth I did enjoy our

collaboration.

ELIJAH. Then why did it stop?

HEDDA. That was your fault /

ELIJAH. You ended it!

HEDDA. Because you ruined it /

ELIJAH. And you ruined me /

HEDDA. Don't you dare blame what happened to you on /

ELIJAH. When you threw me out I had nowhere to go /

HEDDA. You should have thought about that before you did what you did /

ELIJAH. I've been in hell /

HEDDA. Made it ugly, made it cheap, just like everyone else as though I have nothing to offer but /

ELIJAH. You know what your problem is?

Missus. Tesman.

*Beat.*

You're a coward. You're too much of a coward to do

anything.

*The House.*

HEDDA. You're right. I am a coward.

*He chops. They chop.*

Still! You've got Thea collaborating with you now so I'm not sure what you're complaining /

ELIJAH. She told me things. About her childhood. About you.

*Beat.*

HEDDA. And you've told her all about us in return?

ELIJAH. No. She wouldn't understand.

HEDDA. Why?

ELIJAH. She's not like us. She's better than us.

HEDDA. Because I'm a coward... I wonder what you saw in me /

*Doorbell.*

Speak of the devil. (*Calls.*) I'll get it!

*Exit* HEDDA.

ELIJAH *stops chopping.*

*Stares at* HEDDA*'s gin and tonic.*

(*Off.*) Thea! I've been waiting for you all day! Here, I'll take that.

*Takes the glass and holds it level at his eyes.*

*He doesn't want it. He just wants to look at it.*

THEA (*off*). Is Elijah here?

HEDDA (*off*). I've been teaching him how to make the celeriac thing.

*He doesn't want it. He just wants to smell it.*

(*Off.*) Your father and Brack are with The General /

THEA (*off*). Brack? What's Brack /

HEDDA (*off*). And Elijah's in the kitchen…

ELIJAH *puts the glass down.*

*Enter* THEA *and* HEDDA.

THEA. You're here.

ELIJAH. You're here.

*Beat.*

THEA. I'll go and say hello to Dad /

HEDDA. Don't worry about them, they're leaving soon anyway /

THEA. Leaving?

HEDDA. Some party of Brack's. Boys only, very sad /

THEA. You're not going are you?

HEDDA. Elijah's staying with us.

THEA. Good.

HEDDA. Here's a nice cold gin and tonic for you /

THEA. I don't drink alcohol.

HEDDA. You don't?

THEA. How could I? Growing up with you?

*Beat.*

HEDDA. Some warm milk then?

THEA *stands*.

ELIJAH. Isn't she beautiful?

Your daughter.

*Beat.*

HEDDA. Just a pretty face?

ELIJAH. Much more than that. Because we really are collaborators.

HEDDA. Is that so?

ELIJAH. We tell each other everything.

THEA. That's why we can work together, because we trust each other completely.

HEDDA. How nice.

ELIJAH. And she's brave. She's brave enough to do anything.

THEA. I just do what I have to do to live.

ELIJAH. It was her bravery, believing in me when no one else did that helped me get better.

HEDDA. You're sure then, what with all this unremitting bravery in the face of all sorts of various things, that you won't have just one drink with me?

THEA. I said no.

HEDDA. Elijah?

THEA. He can't drink.

HEDDA. But what if I wanted you to?

ELIJAH. Wouldn't make a difference.

HEDDA. So I really have no power over you then?

ELIJAH. Not any more.

HEDDA *continues chopping*.

HEDDA. But I think you should anyway, for your own sake.

THEA. That's the last thing he should do for /

HEDDA. Just in terms of this grand project of yours, what is it? Starting again?

ELIJAH. What about it?

HEDDA. Why should the university trust you when you can't even trust yourself?

THEA. Unlike you we don't care what other people think /

HEDDA. You're right. I do care. Far too much. I guess that's why I felt

ashamed for you. When Brack...

ELIJAH. When Brack what?

HEDDA. It was just a flash. Sort of

contempt.

THEA. Brack's always been contemptuous /

HEDDA. I mean when you were too scared to join them in the other room /

ELIJAH. I wasn't scared! I wanted to talk to you /

HEDDA. Obviously I don't feel this way, we're all much more sensitive about these sorts of things, but that look between George and Brack /

ELIJAH. What look?

HEDDA. I suppose because you won't go to the party, even though it would be good for you really, so many important people /

THEA. It doesn't matter.

HEDDA. So you really are going to stay with me and Thea?

THEA. He is.

ELIJAH. I am.

*Beat.*

HEDDA. Well that is very impressive.

That. Is a man who has the courage of his convictions.
Wouldn't you say, Thea?

*Beat.*

So there was really no need for you to turn up this morning
in such a state /

THEA (*soft*). Hedda!

ELIJAH. What state?

HEDDA. She was practically hysterical Elijah /

THEA. What are you doing!

HEDDA. We hadn't seen her for god knows how long but it
was straight into worrying about you /

ELIJAH. About me?

HEDDA. 'It's not safe for Elijah to be here, please help me stop
him from fucking up his life again' or something like that /

ELIJAH. That's not true /

HEDDA. It is true.

ELIJAH. Thea?

*Beat.*

THEA. Listen to me Elijah /

ELIJAH. But Thea? /

THEA. You have to trust me /

ELIJAH. No you have to trust me!

*Takes* HEDDA*'s glass.*

THEA. No don't do that /

ELIJAH. Here's to you.

*Knocks the drink back.*

*Takes the other glass.*

And here's to the truth. Thanks for the truth Mrs Tesman.

*Knocks the drink back.*

*Goes for a wine bottle.* HEDDA *takes it.*

HEDDA. That's enough for now /

ELIJAH. Fuck you /

HEDDA. You've got the party to go to /

THEA. Are you insane?

HEDDA. Shh! That revolting Brack is watching us.

THEA. Elijah come with me, we can go home tonight /

ELIJAH. You'd like that wouldn't you, keep an eye on me,
control everything I /

THEA. What are you saying /

ELIJAH. Who else have you been talking to?

THEA. No one I promise /

ELIJAH. The university?

THEA. No!

ELIJAH. Tried to convince them not to take me back?

THEA. Of course not /

ELIJAH. Bullshit.

*Grabs at the wine bottle.*

HEDDA. I said that's enough! You have to read your book to
George later /

THEA. No you don't /

ELIJAH. The book.

*Beat.*

Thea I'm sorry I panicked /

THEA. It's okay /

ELIJAH. But don't worry you don't worry because the point is
I'm proving it /

THEA. You don't have to prove anything /

ELIJAH. I do because I need you to believe in me and you lied to me but it's going to be okay /

THEA. I know it is, just /

ELIJAH. I'm here. See? I'm /

THEA. Elijah don't go to the party /

*Enter* BRACK, *followed by* GEORGE.

BRACK. Time's up!

ELIJAH. Yes it is.

THEA. Elijah /

HEDDA. Shh!

*Pinches* THEA. THEA *cries out. Soft.*

BRACK. You're coming?

ELIJAH. If I can?

BRACK. Of course.

ELIJAH. I really want to show George this tonight.

*The book.*

GEORGE. That was all I really wanted.

ELIJAH. I won't stay for long. I'll be back about ten to pick Thea up.

HEDDA. Of course.

GEORGE. Don't expect me back at ten Hedda!

HEDDA. You stay out as long as you like.

THEA. You promise you'll come back?

ELIJAH. I promise.

BRACK. Come on, the taxi's waiting.

THEA. But you promise because I can't be here alone /

ELIJAH. Trust me.

HEDDA. Well have fun, don't do anything I would /

BRACK. I'll tell you all about it tomorrow /

HEDDA. You know how I enjoy hearing about things I'm excluded from.

BRACK. Excluded! Such a strong word…

*GEORGE and BRACK are gone.*

THEA. Elijah!

ELIJAH. At ten. You'll see.

GEORGE (*off*). Elijah!

*ELIJAH is gone.*

*HEDDA pours herself a drink. THEA stares at the doorway.*

THEA. He's not coming back.

HEDDA. Oh relax. Ten o' clock, he'll be here, brave and brilliant and beautiful /

THEA. He's never coming back.

HEDDA. He'll be just like he used to be, his own person and completely free /

THEA. You really have no idea what you've done do you? Oh my god. You actually don't.

HEDDA. You can doubt him but I know him /

THEA. Why are you doing this?

HEDDA. I suppose for the same reason you did what you did to him.

THEA. Which is what?

HEDDA. I want to know what it's like to have power over someone's life.

*Beat.*

THEA. But you already did!

HEDDA. I never did!

THEA. But your own!

HEDDA. Never!

THEA. But you had it all Hedda.

Wasn't that the saying when you were my age?

Having it all?

*Beat.*

Tell me.

What did you do to make such a mess of having it all? What did you do to so catastrophically ruin. The privilege

of Having. It. All.

*Silence. Very sharp.*

HEDDA *to* THEA. THEA *frozen.*

*Enter* BERTHA.

BERTHA. So I've put an overnight wash on /

HEDDA *stops.*

HEDDA *and* THEA *never stop staring at each other.*

Is everything okay?

HEDDA. I thought you'd gone home.

BERTHA. I was about to. I came to say goodnight.

HEDDA. Goodnight.

*Beat.*

BERTHA. What time do I start tomorrow? Is nine okay?

HEDDA. Best make it seven.

BERTHA. Seven?

HEDDA. Lots still to do don't you think?

BERTHA. Okay.

*Beat.*

Night Thea.

THEA. Night.

*Beat.*

*Exit* BERTHA.

*Front door.*

*Silence.*

*Very slowly and with enormous passion* HEDDA *wraps her arms around her daughter.*

HEDDA. Thea. My little girl.

You have no idea how impoverished I've been, how impoverished I have been my entire life.

And you. Allowed to be so rich…

*The House.*

Your hair.

You always had such beautiful hair /

THEA. Mummy let me go I'm frightened /

HEDDA. Maybe I will burn it off /

THEA. I'm frightened Mummy I'm really really frightened /

HEDDA. Maybe I will burn it off after all /

THEA. I have to get out I have to /

HEDDA. You. Are going to sit here and eat your dinner like a good girl. And at ten o clock Elijah will come back, brave and brilliant and beautiful

and then we'll see.

*End of Act Two.*

## ACT THREE

*Dark. Morning behind closed shutters.*

*Stove glowing. Shadows.*

*Mess, gin bottle, wine bottle, untouched meal.*

THEA *sitting, wrapped in a blanket. Her eyes are open.*

THEA*'s phone. Frantic. Picks up.*

THEA. Elijah?

> *Beat.*

> Auntie Julie…

> *Beat.*

> Dad? No I'm not with him.

> I don't know. He went out.

> *Beat.*

> Okay I'll tell him.

> Yes I'll tell him.

> *Beat.*

> I'm fine.

> *Beat.*

> Love you.

> *End call.*

> *The House.*

> *Goes to the stove and puts wood in the stove and stands in the face of its warmth.*

*Front door.*

Elijah?

*Enter* BERTHA.

BERTHA. Morning.

*Opens the shutters. Morning cruel in the room.*

THEA. What time is it?

BERTHA. Just after seven.

*Tidies the table.*

Had a party?

THEA. Hedda did.

BERTHA. Where is she?

THEA. Sleeping. In the sitting room.

BERTHA. Lucky I cleaned her room and everything then.

THEA. She passed out on the sofa.

BERTHA. Hope I'm still doing that when I'm her age /

THEA. It's disgusting.

*Beat.*

BERTHA. Well she's your mum. She's supposed to be embarrassing.

*Pause.*

BERTHA *tidies.* THEA *watches her.*

THEA. Do you have children?

BERTHA. Two. Girl and a boy.

THEA. What are they like?

BERTHA. Like?

Well they're noisy. They make a mess. And they're funny. (*Laughs.*) They say funny things they don't know are funny. Like most kids.

THEA. I wasn't like that.

BERTHA. What were you like?

*Beat.*

THEA. Quiet.

BERTHA. Lucky Hedda.

BERTHA *tidies.*

THEA. Do they. Get in the way?

BERTHA. Of what?

THEA. Everything.

BERTHA. A lot of the time they are everything.

THEA. That's what I mean. How do you do what you want to do?

BERTHA. You mean like passing out on the sofa?

THEA. I mean like work.

BERTHA. I am working.

*Beat.*

BERTHA *tidies.*

Their nan helps out. They're with her now.

THEA. Are they?

BERTHA. I can't take them to school if I'm here can I?

THEA. No…

BERTHA. Mums are useful like that. For a long time you don't know why they're there except to annoy you, and then you have kids and you understand again.

THEA. I'm not going to have kids.

BERTHA. She says it's better being a grandma anyway. You've done it all already so you don't mind.

THEA. Mind what?

BERTHA. Oh just like…

When they hurt themselves, hurt themselves badly, I get so scared…

I'm so scared it's like anger. I think I'd kill them to save them from being hurt.

*Laughs.*

It's crazy how you feel sometimes…

Mum doesn't get scared any more, not like that. She's sad for them 'cause they're hurt but she lets them get on with it. When I was little and did stupid things…

I remember her face. Terror.

THEA. Yes.

BERTHA. Maybe that's what changes. The fear.

BERTHA *finishes tidying.*

THEA. Auntie Julie used to look after me.

BERTHA. Did she?

THEA. She likes looking after people.

BERTHA. Does she?

THEA. I moved in with her till I was old enough to

leave…

BERTHA. Where did you go?

THEA. Not far enough…

BERTHA *goes.*

Do you want a cup of tea or anything?

BERTHA. Thanks, I've had breakfast.

*Exit* BERTHA.

THEA *at a loss. Puts more wood on the stove and stands in the glow.*

*Goes to the garden doors. Sees The General and stops.*

THEA. Hello Grandpa.

*The General doesn't respond.*

*Continues to the doors and looks out at the garden.*

*A door bangs in the house.* HEDDA *wakes bolt upright.*

HEDDA (*panic*). Thea! Where are you?

THEA. I'm here.

*Beat.*

HEDDA. Where are we?

*Enter* HEDDA *from sitting room.*

I remember now.

Strange…

*Beat.*

What time is it?

THEA. Just after seven.

HEDDA. Where's your father?

THEA. Not back.

HEDDA. How extraordinary.

THEA. I told you this would happen.

*Beat.*

HEDDA. Did you sleep?

THEA. No. Yes. I was asleep. But I was awake. And I was trapped.

HEDDA. Your grandfather used to get that. Used to sleepwalk. It would have been ridiculous if it weren't so frightening, this decrepit old man wandering about the house shouting at the clock to stand up straight.

When I was little I'd follow him to make sure he didn't hurt himself. I wasn't allowed in his study but I'd sit with him all night with my tiny cold feet…

Once he tried to strangle me.

I expect he thought I was the enemy…

THEA. You never told me that.

HEDDA. You never asked.

*Pause.*

Thea what's wrong?

THEA. Don't you know what's happened?

HEDDA. I know exactly what's happened. They were up late and didn't want to disturb us so they stayed at Julia's.

THEA. She phoned this morning. She wanted to speak to Dad which means he's not with her.

She didn't say Elijah was there either so /

HEDDA. Then they went to Brack's.

THEA. But /

HEDDA. They've been up all night and Elijah has been reading to your father, reading his brilliant book /

THEA. But he promised he'd come back and get me…

*Beat.*

HEDDA. You know what you need, you need some sleep.

THEA. How could I possibly sleep?

HEDDA. You Will sleep. And you'll feel much better. Go to my room, my bed's made up.

*Beat.*

THEA. Will you wake me if he comes back?

HEDDA. Of course.

*Beat.*

THEA. You need to tell Dad to call Auntie Julie.

HEDDA. I will.

THEA. She said it was urgent.

HEDDA. Go on now.

THEA *goes*.

Thea!

THEA *stops*.

It'll be like when you were little. You'd come into my room in the night and I'd wake up in the morning with you all curled up next to me.

Do you remember?

*Beat.*

THEA. No Hedda. I don't remember that at all.

*Exit* THEA.

HEDDA *and The General*.

HEDDA *pours herself a drink*.

THE GENERAL. She's being a bit of a cunt.

*Beat.*

HEDDA. Sorry?

THE GENERAL. My granddaughter. She is being. A bit. Of a cunt.

*Beat.*

HEDDA. I expect she has her reasons.

THE GENERAL. That'll be your fault. You brought her up.

HEDDA. I'm not so sure I did.

THE GENERAL. Then you're a bit of a cunt too.

HEDDA. What about you?

THE GENERAL. Oh, a tremendous cunt. Unprecedented I should say.

HEDDA. I always thought you were rather great.

THE GENERAL. You see how this works don't you?

Don't you?

*Pause.*

HEDDA. Did you want children?

*The General doesn't respond.*

I don't mean me personally, I'm not trying to get all emotional about this. You were never any good at that. I just mean abstractly, the idea of: Did you want children?

*The General doesn't respond.*

A child?

*The General doesn't respond.*

You see I didn't want children. It just sort of happened and I couldn't bear to think about it and then it was too late…

And they know. The children.

They take it in with your poison

milk.

*Beat.*

Not something you'd understand but all I'm asking, because I wonder whether it's connected, is Did You Want Children?

*The General doesn't respond.*

Daddy?

Daddy?

*Silence.*

HEDDA *to the doors and looks out into the light and the light looks back into her.*

(*Singing, soft.*)

    'Hush little baby don't say a word, mama's gonna buy
      you a mocking bird.

    If that mocking bird don't sing, mama's gonna buy you
      a diamond ring.

    If that diamond ring –

    If that diamond ring…'

*She can't remember the words any more.*

    'So hush little baby don't you cry, your daddy loves you
      and so do I.'

*Just* HEDDA *and the house.*

*Front door.*

*Enter* GEORGE, *tiptoe.*

I can't see you George but I know you look ridiculous.

GEORGE. You're up! /

HEDDA. Don't shout! Thea's asleep upstairs.

*Beat.*

GEORGE. Thea stayed the night?

HEDDA. Of course she did.

And there you were wanting to throw away her bed.

*Beat.*

I couldn't believe it at the time, wanting to throw away your
own daughter's bed.

GEORGE. It wasn't like that Hedda, it was just the cost of
storage /

HEDDA. We'll get Bertha to make up a room. And it will be
her room.

GEORGE. If that's what she wants.

*Beat.*

HEDDA. Why didn't you come home?

GEORGE. I went to Brack's so as not to disturb you.

HEDDA. Well that's ironic because she was very disturbed.

GEORGE. Is Elijah here?

HEDDA. He's not with you?

*They look at each other.*

What happened?

GEORGE. Well we got separated later on in the evening.

HEDDA. But did you have a nice time?

GEORGE. At first. Elijah read to me before the others arrived.
That was the best bit really...

HEDDA. And?

GEORGE. This book Hedda. It's extraordinary.

And I was happy, listening to him, taking notes for him. It
was just like it used to be but then –

Something

came over me. Like a sickness.

HEDDA. Sickness?

GEORGE *laughs*.

GEORGE. I was envious. I've never been envious of anyone
before. It was like hating. It was worse than hating...

You wouldn't understand.

HEDDA. I'm sure I would.

GEORGE. I could never think like that, write like that. And the
stupid thing is it's wasted on him.

HEDDA. How can you say that?

GEORGE. It was my fault. I shouldn't have encouraged him to
go to the party. He's out of control /

HEDDA. Was he brilliant?

GEORGE. Oh sure. But then he became a little

too

brilliant. He just couldn't stop drinking. Gave this great long
embarrassing speech about some woman who inspires him or
something...

I suppose he meant Thea.

HEDDA. I suppose he did.

GEORGE. In the end I thought it'd be best to put him in a cab
back here. Brack and I managed to get him out but the taxis
wouldn't take him, so we were wandering up and down the
road and Elijah was being pretty difficult and –

*Beat.*

You won't believe what I found.

HEDDA. What?

*A dirtied parcel.*

GEORGE. It's his book!

HEDDA. No!

GEORGE. He must have dropped it on the road like it was
rubbish /

HEDDA. Why didn't you give it back to him?

GEORGE. The state he was in! He'd have just lost it again.

HEDDA. Does anyone else know?

GEORGE. I know you think I'm indiscreet Hedda, but I'm not
stupid. He's trying to get back into the university, and to
have drunkenly lost his /

HEDDA. But why didn't you tell him you were going to keep it
safe for him?

GEORGE. I didn't really get to talk to him again.

HEDDA. What do you mean?

GEORGE. He'd got some ridiculous idea into his head that we should all go out. I don't know, he didn't want to stop. Brack thought a cab might be more likely to take him if we booked it, so we called a cab and he became very quiet, quite sweet actually, and…

I suppose we let our guard down a bit.

*Beat.*

And then, quite suddenly, he shouted 'FREEDOM!' and took off down the street.

*Beat.*

HEDDA. He shouted 'freedom' and took off down the street?

GEORGE. Yes exactly. FREEDOM! And just took off. Down the street.

HEDDA. He shouted Freedom and just

ran off…

GEORGE. I'll try and get hold of him now /

HEDDA. No don't! I want to read it.

GEORGE. But he'll be frantic, it's the only copy.

HEDDA. How can it be the Only copy?

GEORGE. It's his first draft, he hasn't typed up yet.

HEDDA. But can't he just write it over again if he's such a genius?

GEORGE. You can't just 'rewrite' things like this Hedda, you know that.

HEDDA. Then that really is it. Right

there…

*Phone.*

Yes I forgot to tell you. Julia phoned.

GEORGE. What did she want?

HEDDA. I don't know, she said you're to call back.

*Exit* GEORGE.

HEDDA *to the book.*

*Phone stops.*

*Looks at it. Picks it up. Very gentle. Holds it to her face.*

*Breathes in.*

Thea...

*Cradles the book. Eyes shut.*

GEORGE (*off*). Hedda!

*She drops the book, steps away.*

*Enter* GEORGE.

HEDDA. I said don't shout /

GEORGE. Auntie Rina's had a stroke. She's in hospital.

HEDDA. Hospital?

GEORGE. I have to go immediately /

HEDDA. Of course /

GEORGE. Will you come with me?

*Beat.*

HEDDA. George you can't ask me /

GEORGE. Hedda please /

HEDDA. I can't have anything to do with hospitals and dying /

GEORGE. But /

HEDDA. Not after Daddy not ever again –

I can't.

I can't.

GEORGE. I know darling /

HEDDA. I'm sorry George I /

GEORGE. I know.

*Beat.*

*Doorbell.*

Now what! It's too much, it's just /

HEDDA. George! The book!

GEORGE. Shit. Give it to –

HEDDA *takes the book to her desk and locks it in the drawer.*

What are you doing?

HEDDA. You can't give it to him now. You've got to go to the hospital.

*Doorbell.*

GEORGE (*shouts*). We're coming!

HEDDA. I'll keep it safe till you get back.

GEORGE. But Hedda /

*Enter* BERTHA *with laundry in a basket.*

BERTHA. That man's at the door.

HEDDA. What man?

BERTHA. The one who likes going for walks in your garden.

HEDDA *to the front door.*

You know you don't have a dryer?

GEORGE. Have you seen my other shoe?

BERTHA. Your shoe?

GEORGE. I need my shoe. It's very important.

BERTHA. Okay.

*She puts down the basket and they look for his shoe.*

HEDDA (*off*). Brack! Front door today is it?

BRACK (*off*). You've locked your garden gate on me.

*They come into the kitchen.*

HEDDA (*off*). The early bird gets the locked –

What on earth are you both doing?

*They are crawling around on the floor.*

BERTHA. Morning Hedda. I was just saying, you don't have a dryer.

HEDDA. But why would this house have anything so sensible as a dryer...

GEORGE. Got it!

*The shoe.*

BERTHA. There's a line in the garden but it looks like rain...

BRACK. George are you alright?

GEORGE. Auntie Rina's had a stroke.

BRACK. I'm so sorry. Please, don't worry about me /

GEORGE. I won't.

*Exit* GEORGE.

*Front door.*

*Beat.*

BERTHA. I'm sorry his aunt's had a stroke.

HEDDA. Unfortunately it's just what she does these days...

By the way, the room at the end, could you make up the bed?

BERTHA. Sure.

HEDDA. My daughter's staying for a bit.

BERTHA. I'll unpack the boxes as well then?

HEDDA. Thank you.

BERTHA. What should I do with the washing?

HEDDA. Oh I don't know. Burn it.

BERTHA. Okay.

*Exit* BERTHA *with laundry.*

BRACK. I don't know how you can say you're bored. It's been non-stop excitement ever since you got here.

HEDDA. And speaking of excitement, I hear you had your fair share last night.

BRACK. What's Professor Tesman been telling you?

HEDDA. Just that you spent your evening walking up and down the road or something equally /

BRACK. Did he mention Elijah was with us?

HEDDA. He might have mentioned that.

BRACK. And did he mention that Elijah was then, quite suddenly, not with us?

HEDDA. He might have mentioned that too.

*Pause.*

*Smiles.*

He's not here Brack.

BRACK. I know he's not here.

*Beat.*

HEDDA. Where is he?

BRACK. He's in a cell.

HEDDA. What do you mean 'a cell'?

BRACK. A holding cell, at the police station.

*Beat.*

HEDDA. You're lying.

BRACK. I am not.

*Beat.*

HEDDA. Will they let him out?

BRACK. When he is sober and poses no threat to the public.

*Beat.*

HEDDA. How do you know this?

BRACK. Because I have spoken to the police.

HEDDA. Why?

BRACK. Because Elijah included me and my party in his version of last night's events.

HEDDA. And what else was included in his version of last night's events?

BRACK. As far as I understand he went from bar to bar buying rounds of drinks for everyone he /

HEDDA. Entire bars?

BRACK. Until the staff decided he was too inebriated and threw him out. At which point he'd move on to the next one and then the next one and /

HEDDA. That's absurd, he can't afford that /

BRACK. Exactly. In the last bar he was unable to pay. But the drinks had been drunk and as you can imagine the staff weren't very pleased.

HEDDA. Yes I can imagine that...

BRACK. During the argument his behaviour changed quite violently. He became angry, panicked, claimed he had lost something and tried to leave the bar. The staff wouldn't let him go until he paid for the drinks, he accused them of stealing from him, a fight ensued, the police were called and he resisted arrest and hit a police officer.

*Beat.*

HEDDA. What does that mean?

BRACK. Dependent on aggravating factors, assaulting a police officer incurs a maximum sentence of six months in prison and up to a five-thousand-pound fine.

HEDDA. Oh.

BRACK. Yes. Oh.

*Beat.*

HEDDA. No such thing as starting again…

BRACK. Now none of this need concern you /

HEDDA. And it doesn't, I don't want to hear anything more about /

BRACK. I'm afraid you have to because this rather affects us.

HEDDA. 'Us' is it?

BRACK. I'd like to think so.

HEDDA. You can think what you like but this has nothing to do with /

BRACK. Elijah will want to use you, George and Thea as character witnesses.

HEDDA. Then let him.

BRACK. I would advise against that.

HEDDA. And why would you offer such scintillating legal advice?

BRACK. Because I think you should cut yourself off from Elijah altogether.

HEDDA. But I like Elijah.

*Beat.*

He's

how did we put it? Fun. Interesting. Nothing academic about him, in the usual sense /

BRACK. I would find it extremely unpleasant if Elijah were to join us in our train carriage.

HEDDA. Would you?

BRACK. Three is enough for a pleasant journey, don't you think? Any more than that and I might start to feel

crowded.

*Beat.*

HEDDA. What a funny little man you are Brack.

*Laughs.*

Always have been.

*Beat.*

BRACK. None of this should matter anyway. From where I'm standing, or sitting as you said yourself, in judgement on people's lives, I'd be surprised if Elijah managed to avoid prison.

*The House.*

You see how this works, don't you?

Don't you?

HEDDA *stands.*

BRACK *stands, as a coincidence, but now he is blocking her way.*

*Beat.*

HEDDA. You know, sometimes you remind me of my father.

BRACK. High praise, from you.

HEDDA. You actually think you're dangerous don't you?

BRACK. I do.

HEDDA. Fine. Be dangerous. Just don't try putting your hands around my neck.

BRACK. No, you wouldn't want that.

HEDDA. And you won't want to forget that I can be quite dangerous too.

When the mood takes me.

BRACK *smiles*.

HEDDA *smiles*.

BRACK *starts to go via the garden*.

Sneaking out the back again?

BRACK. I've always enjoyed coming and going via the back entrance.

HEDDA. Even during target practice?

BRACK. We don't shoot our friends do we Hedda?

HEDDA. Not unless we have a surplus.

*Beat.*

*Exit* BRACK.

*She watches him go.*

*The smile drops from her face.*

*Goes and puts more wood in the stove. Stands in the face of its warmth.*

*Goes and looks in the sitting room. Sees The General.*

Oh shut up.

*The General doesn't respond.*

*Goes to her desk, unlocks the drawer and takes out the book.*

*Holds it.*

*Sits and reads.*

*Silence.*

*Doorbell.*

*Looks up.*

BERTHA (*off*). I'll get it!

*Pause.*

*Front door.*

ELIJAH (*off*). I need to come in /

HEDDA *stands.*

BERTHA (*off*). What are you /

ELIJAH (*off*). Move!

HEDDA *locks the book away.*

BERTHA (*off*). I'll call the police!

ELIJAH (*off*). 'I'll call the police!'

*Enter* ELIJAH, *followed by* BERTHA.

*Freezes, looking at* HEDDA, *her looking at him.*

*He is a ruin.*

BERTHA. I tried to stop him /

HEDDA. It's okay /

BERTHA. But he just pushed past /

HEDDA. It's okay Bertha.

BERTHA. He's not safe.

HEDDA. Neither am I.

ELIJAH *laughs.*

*Beat.*

BERTHA. I'm just upstairs. If you need me.

*Exit* BERTHA.

*Pause.*

HEDDA. You're late.

ELIJAH. Where's Thea?

*Beat.*

You won't tell me.

You're afraid for her. You should be.

Where's George?

*Beat.*

HEDDA. Upstairs in bed.

ELIJAH. What did he tell you?

HEDDA. That you had a very nice /

ELIJAH. Liar!

*Beat.*

One of you is. Shall we play a game?

HEDDA. Okay.

ELIJAH. The Who's Lying game.

HEDDA. Okay.

ELIJAH. So who's lying? Hedda Tesler or Dr George? Hedda Gahb-Man or /

*Enter* THEA.

THEA. Elijah!

ELIJAH. You're here /

THEA. Of course I'm here /

ELIJAH. You waited /

THEA. Of course I waited.

*Beat.*

ELIJAH. I'm sorry.

*Pause.*

HEDDA. Should I /

ELIJAH. Don't move!

We all need to stay exactly /

THEA. You're drunk.

ELIJAH. No.

Yes.

Maybe. One. On the way.

Two…

THEA. Okay time to go /

ELIJAH. Where?

THEA. Away from here /

ELIJAH. I can't get away from here /

THEA. Elijah /

ELIJAH. Don't touch me!

*Beat.*

I'm going to tell you everything and then /

THEA. I don't want to know, I just want to get out of /

ELIJAH. You're not Listening there's nowhere else to –

Get the fuck away from me!

HEDDA. Thea come over here /

THEA. Shut up Hedda I know how to deal with this!

HEDDA *moves.*

ELIJAH. You stay there!

HEDDA *freezes.*

I need you there.

I need you both to –

*Beat.*

Wait…

*He thinks.*

That's it.

(*To* THEA.) You.

Go home.

THEA. What do you mean?

ELIJAH. Go back to your husband /

THEA. I don't have a husband /

ELIJAH. Go back and

I don't know.

Live. If you have to.

THEA. You don't say that to me /

ELIJAH. It's over Thea /

THEA. You don't say that because we have work to do /

ELIJAH. I don't need you any more /

THEA. Everything will be okay when the book's published /

ELIJAH. It's not going to be /

THEA. And we're going to write more books and /

ELIJAH. It's not going to /

THEA. It is /

ELIJAH. It isn't /

THEA. It /

ELIJAH. Isn't!

*Beat.*

THEA. Elijah where's the book /

ELIJAH. Don't ask me /

THEA. Tell me where it is I have a right to know I –

Now.

*Beat.*

ELIJAH. The book. Yes.

The thing about the book is –

*Giggles.*

I destroyed it.

HEDDA (*at once*). That's not –

THEA (*at once*.) You're lying!

ELIJAH. I never lie! I tore it up!

THEA. He tore up our work all our work /

ELIJAH. I tore it page by page. First I tore one page. And then I tore another page. And I tore all the pages into a thousand pieces down by the docks and I scattered them in the water. And they'll drift in the water and they'll drift out to sea where it's clean and salt and deep and then

they'll sink.

Deeper and deeper deeper and deeper just like me…

*Pause.*

THEA. Do you know what you've done?

ELIJAH. Yes.

THEA. All of my life, for the rest of my life it will be like you killed a little child /

ELIJAH. Yes.

THEA. But it was my child too…

*Beat.*

ELIJAH. Was it?

*Beat.*

You carried it for me. But it's not like you have any thoughts.

*The words sit in the room.*

THEA. I'm going now.

HEDDA. Going where?

THEA. I don't know.

It's all just

dark. Under the surface.

*She starts to go.*

HEDDA. Don't go!

THEA *stops.*

You can stay here.

We've got your bed, you remember your old bed? We kept it we –

So you see, you can stay here with /

THEA. I don't think that's going to work Hedda.

You didn't want me when I was born. You didn't want me my entire life, don't pretend you want me now. Just because you're bored don't pretend to yourself that you want me now.

*Exit* THEA.

*Front door.*

*Silence.*

ELIJAH. Hedda

Gah-blah.

*She is looking at his hand. He follows her gaze. It trembles.*

*A leaf.*

*He goes to the table and pours the rest of the gin and drinks it and is calmed.*

HEDDA. Feeling better now?

*He laughs.*

ELIJAH. I've ruined my life.

Again.

HEDDA. Yes well. Haven't we all.

ELIJAH. Were the odds stacked against us? Or are we

rotten.

Inside.

HEDDA. I really don't know any more.

*Beat.*

ELIJAH. I could have burned out long ago. I felt so bright all

the time. Rushing. Crackling. Fire…

Your daughter turned up and put it out. I thought she'd saved
me but she's

ruined me.

HEDDA. You really think that disturbed little girl had so much
power over /

ELIJAH. Who ruined you?

*Beat.*

HEDDA. That's why you were so cruel.

ELIJAH. Cruel?

HEDDA. About the book.

ELIJAH. I can tell you the truth.

HEDDA. So you did lie.

ELIJAH. To protect her.

She said what I did was like killing a child. But there are
worse things a father can do to his child than killing it.

HEDDA. And what do you know about what fathers can do to
their children?

*Beat.*

ELIJAH. Imagine a man who has gone out at night. Gone out
all night.

And this man goes to places where children shouldn't go and does things that children shouldn't see.

And he takes his child by the hand and takes the child with him and somewhere

in the night he

lets go…

And in the morning he goes back to the child's mother and says, 'The child is lost. I've lost our child. I don't know where she is or who she's with or what they're doing to' /

HEDDA. It's just a book! It's not a child it isn't a child it's a /

ELIJAH. Thea's whole Life was in that book. So you see there's no future for us.

HEDDA. Whatever you say, Professor.

ELIJAH. Please don't call me that.

*Beat.*

*He clutches his head, slowly, and crouches down.*

I can't do this again.

*Stands.*

It won't stop with last night. It's got its claws in me and it's going to eat me and I can't do it again because I don't

know how.

HEDDA. What are you going to do?

ELIJAH. End it.

*Beat.*

You won't try and stop me?

HEDDA. Why should I? I respect your choice. And I respect you for making it.

*Beat.*

ELIJAH. You are miraculous.

*Beat.*

HEDDA. I don't think

that it is possible for us to live beautifully. But I do think that
it's possible. I think that it has to be possible to die.
Beautifully.

ELIJAH (*smiles*). And bravely and brilliantly, like you used to
say?

HEDDA. And would you promise me. That you will?

ELIJAH. Yes.

HEDDA. Then I have something for you.

*Goes to the gun case and gets one of the guns and brings it
to him.*

ELIJAH *looks at it.*

ELIJAH. Your dad's?

*He takes the gun. She holds on to it.*

HEDDA. His man's. He loved him, but he was killed. In Egypt.

*She lets go of the gun.*

Something to remember me by anyway. At the end.

*Beat.*

ELIJAH. Will you tell George I'm sorry. Tell him I'm sorry that
I couldn't –

HEDDA. Yes.

ELIJAH. Bye then.

Hedda Gabler.

*Exit* ELIJAH.

*Front door.*

*She looks after him a long time.*

HEDDA *and The General alone.*

*Goes to the desk and takes out the book. Looks at the book.*

*Beat.*

*Goes to the stove and kneels down and opens the door and she tears off a page and puts the page in.*

*It flares up. And is gone.*

*Tears off another page and puts it in.*

*It flares up. And is gone.*

*Tears off more pages and puts them in and they flare up. And are gone.*

HEDDA. I'm burning your child Thea.

*More pages and so on.*

Your and Elijah's child.

*She puts the rest of the book in and the light burns on her face.*

Now I'm burning it. I'm burning the child.

*End of Act Three.*

**ACT FOUR**

*Lights. Evening. Rain.*

HEDDA *playing the piano in the sitting room.*

BERTHA *in the kitchen. Empties the ashes from the stove into a metal bucket and takes it out.*

BERTHA. I'm off now.

    HEDDA *stops playing.*

HEDDA (*off*). Okay Bertha. See you next week.

BERTHA. You going to be alright?

    HEDDA *playing again.*

    *Exit* BERTHA.

    *Front door.*

    HEDDA *playing. A while.*

    *Key in the lock. Front door.*

    *Shuffling.*

    JULIE *there watching her play through the sitting-room door.*

    HEDDA *stops. Runs over a mistake. Tries again. Stops. Runs over a mistake. Tries again. Stops.*

JULIE. It's so nice to hear you play.

    *Beat.*

You used to play so well and we never hear you play any more.

    *Beat.*

HEDDA *in the doorway. A black suit.*

HEDDA. How did you get in?

JULIE. I had a set of keys made.

HEDDA. Of course you did.

*Beat.*

JULIE. I remember that suit. You were wearing it the day
we met.

HEDDA. Daddy had just died.

JULIE. So few people wear black these days. A proper
upbringing. That's what I thought the moment I saw you.

*Beat.*

HEDDA. Have you ever felt like a piece of thick meat?
Squeezed into too fine a skin? Like a

sausage. Say.

A proper sausage. Not some shit sausage that's half-water
and half-nothing, a sausage that's all meat and flavour, ready
to burst open and split its skin when it's heated up?

*Beat.*

JULIE. I can't say I've ever felt like that.

*Pause.*

HEDDA. I am so very sorry for your loss. If there's anything
I can do…

JULIE. No Hedda dear. George has explained to me, about your
father. You mustn't even think about it.

HEDDA. Thoughts aren't so easily mastered…

JULIE. At least she's not in pain now.

HEDDA. Was it hard? When she –

JULIE. Oh no. It was very gentle.

I would even say it was beautiful.

HEDDA. Beautiful?

JULIE. She hadn't moved all morning but when George came she knew him and she raised her arm. The effort was huge for her but she raised her arm and touched his cheek.

HEDDA. Did she look. Pleased?

JULIE. Pleased?

No. She looked happy.

*The House.*

HEDDA. I don't suppose you've seen Thea today?

JULIE. I thought she was here?

HEDDA. She is here.

She's not here right now. But she is fundamentally. Here.

*Beat.*

We've made a room up for her.

JULIE. She's come home?

*Beat.*

I was saying to George, just yesterday, that it's all you were lacking /

HEDDA. Yes.

JULIE. It makes sense of Auntie Rina's passing.

HEDDA. How's that?

JULIE. But Hedda, this is why we die. So the young people can live.

*Front door.*

*Enter* GEORGE.

GEORGE. Look at you both.

*Goes to kiss his aunt.*

JULIE. Did you get everything done?

GEORGE. No...

I'm a little distracted. You never think how much there is to manage...

JULIE. You should be happy for her. For a life well lived.

HEDDA. But you'll be lonely now Julia.

JULIE. I don't think so. I have a spare room to fill.

GEORGE. Really? Who would you want to take it?

JULIE. There's always some poor person who needs a place to be.

HEDDA. You want to burden yourself with a stranger?

JULIE. Strangers don't stay strange for long. And now that we're all together again, we can take such good care of each other.

HEDDA. Oh, please don't worry about us.

GEORGE. Will you stay for dinner?

JULIE. I only came to check in on Hedda.

GEORGE. You are sweet /

JULIE. You said yourself, death is so hard for her /

GEORGE. Yes, that's true /

JULIE. And the thought of her out here, all alone /

HEDDA. Goodnight Aunt Julie.

*Beat.*

JULIE. George! She called me Aunt!

HEDDA. I didn't /

GEORGE. You did Hedda! /

HEDDA. Please don't fuss!

JULIE. We won't fuss. We just love you so much.

*Hugs her.*

HEDDA *stiff.*

Goodnight dear.

GEORGE *walks her out.*

We have to choose Auntie Rina's clothes.

GEORGE. I'll come round first thing in the morning.

JULIE (*off*). She'll go to her grave looking beautiful, just like Hedda.

*Front door.*

*Beat.*

HEDDA. Fuck.

*Beat.*

*Enter* GEORGE.

GEORGE. Well then.

*Takes off his shoes.*

Bit chilly isn't it?

*Puts his shoes back on.*

*Goes to the cold stove.*

*Pokes it thoughtfully with his foot.*

HEDDA. You're taking this even harder than Julia.

GEORGE. It's not just Auntie Rina. It's Elijah.

HEDDA. What about Elijah?

GEORGE. I can't get hold of him.

*Beat.*

I've been trying all day, I wanted to let him know we've got the book but...

HEDDA. He's probably sleeping /

GEORGE. I called Thea and she said he was here.

   This morning.

   *Beat.*

HEDDA. So?

GEORGE. She said he said he'd torn up the book.

HEDDA. So?

GEORGE. But why would he say that! Thea was distraught /

HEDDA. He said all sorts of things, he was in a state.

GEORGE. So that's why you didn't give it back to him?

HEDDA. Something like that.

GEORGE. But you reassured him we had it?

HEDDA. No.

GEORGE. No!

HEDDA. Did you tell Thea?

   *Beat.*

GEORGE. No… I wasn't sure whether…

   *Goes to the desk. Searches the drawer and the desktop.*

   You better give it to me now though and I'll try and find him.
   He'll be desperate, what if he does something stupid? Well
   you know what he could be like – these bloody guns! – for
   god's sake Hedda where is it?

HEDDA. I don't have it any more.

GEORGE. What do you mean you 'don't have it any more'?

HEDDA. I burnt it.

GEORGE. What do you mean you 'burnt it'?

   HEDDA *points to the stove.*

   *Beat.*

Burnt like –

You mean actually burnt –

Elijah's book you burnt it!

*Goes to the stove and opens the door and looks inside.*

How could you do that? How could you even think it? Are you insane?

*Beat.*

(*Shout.*) Answer me!

HEDDA. I did it for you.

GEORGE. For me?

HEDDA. This morning when you said you envied him /

GEORGE. But I didn't mean /

HEDDA. I know what it's like to

want something that someone else has. To lack something. Fundamental.

*Beat.*

I just wanted you to be happy. I'd do anything for you to be happy.

*Pause.*

GEORGE. Is that what it's like?

So violent? Love.

*Beat.*

But still it's –

*Beat.*

I never knew you loved me like that.

I never knew you loved me at all.

*Pause of thirty years between them.*

*He goes and kneels down by her and holds her body.*

*Her face does something strange and complex but he doesn't see.*

Hedda Hedda Hedda Hedda...

You haven't lived the life you wanted to live /

HEDDA. Don't George /

GEORGE. Let me say this because we don't know how to talk to each other and have never known how to talk about certain /

HEDDA. I don't want to talk about /

GEORGE. I don't know how the choices we made got in the way, I've been afraid to look. But it's going to be alright /

HEDDA. It's always been alright George /

GEORGE. It hasn't but we will be rich. We will be rich in what we have and what we've made because you love me and I love you and I've never loved anyone like I've loved Hedda Tesman.

*Pause.*

HEDDA. Can you hear the rain? In the garden.

It's like praying.

*Silence. And the rain.*

THEA *outside the garden doors and bangs on the glass.*

HEDDA *cries out.*

*She has seen a ghost.*

GEORGE. Thea!

*Opens the doors.*

What are you /

THEA. I'm sorry I'm sorry the gate was open so I /

GEORGE. You're soaked /

THEA. It doesn't matter /

HEDDA. What's happened to you /

GEORGE. It's Elijah isn't it?

THEA. Something's happened I know something's happened
I went to his hotel /

HEDDA. After how he treated you?

THEA. I had to talk to him about the book but he wasn't there
and they said he hadn't been there since yesterday /

GEORGE. Yesterday!

THEA. And I think I'm going to die of not knowing I think I'm
going to /

GEORGE. Right. I'll call the police /

HEDDA. Don't you get mixed up in this /

GEORGE. I have a responsibility, a responsibility to /

*Doorbell.*

*They all stop.*

GEORGE *goes.*

HEDDA, THEA *and The General.*

*Front door.*

(*Off.*) Brack! This is /

BRACK (*off*). I'm sorry it's late but /

GEORGE (*off*). Yes, it's just that we're slightly /

BRACK (*off*). I needed to speak to you immediately /

*Enter* BRACK *and* GEORGE.

THEA. Tell him to go away!

GEORGE. She's a little upset /

THEA. I am not a little upset! I'm /

HEDDA. Has something happened?

THEA. It's Elijah I know it's /

BRACK. What gave you that idea?

*She doesn't answer.*

Have you heard something?

GEORGE. For god's sake Brack just /

BRACK. Well. Elijah died at the hospital this / afternoon

HEDDA (*a breath*). So quick!

THEA. I have to see him /

GEORGE. Thea!

BRACK. You can't see him. No one can see him /

THEA. I have to /

BRACK. I'm sorry.

*Beat.*

GEORGE. He didn't

himself, did he?

HEDDA. He did…

BRACK. Correct. Hedda.

THEA. No he couldn't /

GEORGE. Himself! Awful!

THEA. Where was he?

GEORGE. Thea…

THEA. I need to see it I need to be with him there where was he?

*Beat.*

BRACK. In his hotel room.

THEA. No he wasn't.

*Beat.*

BRACK. Somewhere else then. All I know is that he shot himself in the head /

HEDDA. In the head?

BRACK. In the head /

THEA. It's true. It's gone. Gone

gone

gone

gone

*Methodically and rapidly starts hitting the side of her head with her fist.*

HEDDA. George stop her I can't do it again I can't /

THEA. Gone

gone

GEORGE *struggles to contain* THEA, *brings her to the floor.*

HEDDA *covers her face.*

gone

gone

gone

gone

*Etc.*

*Eventually she is still.*

*Silence.*

BRACK *staring.*

I'm in control now.

Can you let me go now?

Can you let me go?

GEORGE *stands, careful.*

THEA *sits on the floor.*

*Pause.*

HEDDA. I think. What we all need to consider is that there is
something beautiful about /

GEORGE. Beautiful!

BRACK. Hedda!

HEDDA. Some people are not made for this world. Or this
world is not made for them. And then the only honest thing
you can do is say

no more. Of this /

THEA. How can you think that?

HEDDA. Because to me

it is brave. And beautiful /

GEORGE. It's the opposite of brave /

HEDDA. There's a room and it's filling up with water. You can
sink or you can swim but your arms are so tired...

They've never ached like this and you know that if you just

sink. You'll find peace there. In the water.

THEA. It wasn't like that. It was being back here. It made him
sick, like when he tore up the book.

BRACK. What do you mean?

THEA. Last night. He tore it up.

GEORGE. That's the worst thing. Elijah's gone, and we don't
even have his book to remember him by.

THEA. But I'm going to rewrite it.

GEORGE. I'd give anything to do that but /

THEA. Then why don't we?

*Beat.*

GEORGE. Thea darling you can't /

THEA. It wasn't just his. You all keep

saying that. But it was my book too. We wrote it together, we talked about everything together. When his hands shook he'd dictate to me, and I recorded all our conversations.

It's just raw material but if we worked together I could reconstruct it.

GEORGE. It would be difficult /

THEA. I have to try.

GEORGE. And it wouldn't be the same /

THEA. Why does it have to be exactly the same?

GEORGE. You mean start over, from the beginning?

THEA. I need to do this and I need you to help me.

Will you help me?

*Beat.*

GEORGE. Yes /

THEA. You will /

GEORGE. If it's what you need then yes, yes you're right. My own material can wait.

HEDDA. Your own material, George?

GEORGE. You understand don't you Hedda?

HEDDA. What I understand is that your new position requires you to produce work of your own. Not edit someone else's /

GEORGE. Then I won't accept the position.

HEDDA. So we're back to where we were yesterday. Except now by choice, you're throwing it away by /

GEORGE. I've never been a great mind.

I've always known that, really. But I am

a good teacher and I care about my field. I care about the past. And I care, deeply, for the future.

THEA. And this book is the future.

*Beat.*

Can we start right away?

GEORGE. You mean right now?

THEA. Right now.

*They start to go.*

GEORGE. What do you need?

THEA. Your laptop. We'll have to transcribe...

*Exit* THEA *and* GEORGE.

*Later, they go into the sitting room and sit at the table with the laptop and, watched by The General, they do the work.*

HEDDA. Doesn't it make you feel...

BRACK. What?

HEDDA. Complete and perfect release.

BRACK. Why?

HEDDA. That it is possible to do something, really do something of your own free will.

BRACK. Free will?

HEDDA. To make an Actual Choice to

check out of this rotting feast we call living, and be brave enough to die. Beautifully.

*Beat.*

BRACK. I hate to disillusion you but Elijah didn't die of his 'own free will'. And the accident certainly wasn't beautiful.

HEDDA. What do you mean 'accident'?

BRACK. Considering the state Thea was in, I thought it best to avoid some of the more

ugly details.

HEDDA. Ugly?

BRACK. What I've gathered is that late this afternoon he returned to the bar where he was arrested /

HEDDA. There? What was he doing /

BRACK. He was raving about something he'd lost, threatened a woman with a gun /

HEDDA. He didn't! /

BRACK. He did. Seemed confused. Kept talking about a child...

I thought he meant his book. But Thea tells us he destroyed the book. So it couldn't be that.

HEDDA *laughs soft*.

HEDDA. And I imagined him by the water...

BRACK. No water. Just the bar and the woman and the discharged gun /

HEDDA. And the wound in his head.

BRACK. Head? No. That was another amended detail for Thea's sake. In fact, he shot his own cock off.

*Beat*.

You see, he rather stupidly had the gun in his waistband.

HEDDA. His /

BRACK. Cock. Yes. Penis, Hedda. Testicles too by all accounts /

HEDDA. That's disgusting!

Everything I touch, everything I've ever tried to do becomes ridiculous and ugly and –

Do you think I'm toxic?

BRACK. I can't comment on that. But there is something that concerns you directly /

HEDDA. I don't want anything more to do with /

BRACK. This won't take long.

*Beat.*

The gun, or, more accurately, service revolver…

He must have stolen it.

HEDDA. He didn't!

BRACK. I think he did /

HEDDA. Elijah would never /

BRACK. I think. You'll find. That it is the only possible / explanation.

*Laptop next door bursts into life.*

ELIJAH'S VOICE. Because nothing happens that has not already happened /

THEA'S VOICE. And everything that happens is contained in its past.

ELIJAH'S VOICE. If you can trace events, their roots, the trajectories of roots then you can begin to predict outcomes.

THEA'S VOICE. We're talking about inheritance.

ELIJAH'S VOICE. And ghosts…

*Beat.*

THEA'S VOICE. Are we doing that thing where we go off on tangents?

*Laughter.*

*The laptop cuts.*

*Silence.*

BRACK. As I was saying, he must have stolen the gun.

HEDDA. Why?

BRACK. Because any other explanation would be completely inconceivable to me.

HEDDA. You always did lack imagination /

BRACK. He was with you this morning.

HEDDA. Yes.

BRACK. In here?

HEDDA. Yes.

BRACK. You were alone with him?

HEDDA. Yes.

BRACK. And did you leave the room at any point?

HEDDA. No.

BRACK. Did you leave the room at any point Hedda?

*Beat.*

HEDDA. Maybe I. Went out, just for a minute /

BRACK. And where was The General's gun case during this time?

HEDDA. In the sitting room /

BRACK. Where was The General's gun case during this time?

HEDDA. Where it is now.

BRACK. On your desk?

HEDDA. On my desk.

BRACK. And have you checked it since to see if both guns are there?

HEDDA. No.

BRACK. And you won't have to. Because I know both guns are not there. I know both guns are not there because I know Elijah had one this afternoon. And I know Elijah had one this afternoon because I recognised it and I recognised it because you had some fun shooting at me yesterday.

*Beat.*

Funny how these things turn out /

HEDDA. Do you have it?

BRACK. I don't.

HEDDA. Who has it?

BRACK. The police of course.

HEDDA. What will they do with it?

BRACK. They will try to trace the owner.

HEDDA. Good luck to them.

BRACK. It shouldn't be hard. I remember being told that the guns were licensed.

*Beat.*

I'd hate for them not to be licensed. Illegal possession of firearms, that would be a very serious matter.

HEDDA *stares into the dark of the stove.*

HEDDA. Will they. Find me.

BRACK. Not if I keep quiet.

HEDDA. And if you don't?

BRACK. We can discuss illegal possession of firearms at a later date. The other matter which we'll resolve very happily now is you'll be able to say Elijah stole the gun.

HEDDA. I'd rather die.

BRACK. People like to say things like that. They don't really mean it.

HEDDA. Why should I say he stole it?

BRACK. But Hedda! Just imagine if it came out that you gave Elijah the gun, willingly gave him the gun when he was in that state? What would George think? What would Thea think? What would everyone think of a woman who gave a man in such a state a gun?

*Beat.*

And I suppose people might begin to wonder what such a woman's intentions might have been.

*Beat.*

This will all come up at the trial of course.

HEDDA. Trial?

BRACK. Was it accidental death? Or manslaughter? Or

murder?

The woman he threatened will be called. I'd be so interested to see how you both respond to cross-examination. She'll have to go through everything. How did the gun go off? Was it really an accident? Was there a struggle and she got the gun off him? Did she defend herself and then put it back in his waistband /

HEDDA. Stop talking you have to stop talking /

BRACK. How familiar with Elijah's waistband are you Mrs Tesman? How many waistbands of how many Elijahs have you been familiar with over the years Mrs Tesman /

HEDDA. Why are you doing this?

BRACK. And you say *I* lack imagination.

*She laughs. It chokes.*

HEDDA. My neck… You've got me by the neck…

BRACK. I don't want to abuse my position Hedda.

HEDDA. No I can't be trapped like this not now not like this /

BRACK. I think it's amazing what people can get used to /

HEDDA. I have to get out /

*She stands. Simultaneously:*

GEORGE (*calls*). Hedda?

*She freezes.*

*Enter* GEORGE.

BRACK. How goes the Great Elijah Memorial Project?

GEORGE. We're making a start. It's just that my study's full of boxes...

Hedda?

HEDDA. Oh.

GEORGE. I suppose Bertha hasn't got round to it yet.

HEDDA. Oh.

GEORGE. The thing is, it's quite uncomfortable in the sitting room. The table's too low and I'm worried I'm going to damage my back.

HEDDA. Oh...

*Beat.*

GEORGE. I wanted to ask if we could use your desk until my study's set up.

*She stares at him.*

*Finally:*

HEDDA. Certainly George. What's mine is yours, and ever shall be.

GEORGE. Thanks Hedda.

HEDDA. Please, let me tidy it for you.

*Gathers the gun case and her papers and takes them into the sitting room.*

GEORGE (*calls*). Thea?

*Enter* THEA.

*They colonise* HEDDA*'s desk.*

THEA. This is much better.

HEDDA *comes back in and goes to* THEA *and strokes her hair.*

HEDDA. Doesn't it feel strange? Working with your daddy the way you used to work with Elijah?

THEA. No. I was born to do this.

HEDDA. That's nice. I don't know what I was born to do.

THEA *shrugs* HEDDA *off, distracted.*

GEORGE. There is an overwhelming amount of material…

HEDDA. Maybe I could help? It was my field too after all /

THEA. We're fine.

GEORGE. Why don't you go and keep Brack company?

BRACK. Yes Hedda, come and keep me company.

*Beat.*

HEDDA (*the smallest of small voices*). Are you sure there isn't something I could do for you?

Anything at all?

THEA. We just need to concentrate.

GEORGE. You don't mind keeping Hedda entertained, do you Brack?

BRACK. It would be my pleasure.

HEDDA *to sitting room.*

*Beat.*

*Loud, on the piano, Julius Fucik, 'Entry of the Gladiators'.*

THEA. Now what's she doing!

GEORGE. Hedda don't!

THEA. We're trying to work!

GEORGE. And it's not appropriate, think of Elijah, and Auntie Rina /

HEDDA (*off*). And Auntie Julie! And Daddy! And all the rest of them!

*Stops playing.*

(*Off.*) Okay. I'll be quiet from now on. Completely. Quiet.

*Pause.*

GEORGE. I don't think it's good for her. Seeing us doing this.

THEA. No I know. It's difficult…

*Beat.*

I could. Go and live with Auntie Julie again?

GEORGE. She'd love that!

THEA. I'd like that too.

GEORGE. I could come round in the evenings, or you'd come to my office /

HEDDA (*off*). I can hear what you're saying and it's completely ridiculous.

HEDDA *in the doorway.*

She's not going to live with Auntie fucking Julie. She's going to live here, with me, where she belongs.

THEA. I don't want to live here.

*Beat.*

HEDDA. But I kept your bed for you.

THEA. I don't want that old bed.

*Beat.*

GEORGE. It might be for the best Hedda, just all things considered…

*They go back to work.*

HEDDA *alone.*

HEDDA. And what am I supposed to do? Night after night out here in the middle of nowhere?

GEORGE. I'm sure Brack will be happy to visit.

BRACK. Every evening if I can manage it. We'll have a great time, just the two of us.

*She laughs. Short. Sharp. In wonder.*

HEDDA. I think I may have made a mistake.

Somewhere along the line.

*Gun, quick, to her chin.*

*Shot.*

*She falls.*

*And no one there to catch her.*

*Simultaneously:*

*Lights out except* THEA *and The General.*

THEA *stands. She knows.*

*And:*

GEORGE. She's playing with those bloody guns again, I've told her and told her /

THEA *screams.*

Hedda? Hedda! Brack she's shot herself!

BRACK. But she's /

GEORGE. Shot herself in the head Brack call an ambulance!

BRACK. But people don't do things like that!

*Blackout.*

*End of Act Four.*

**Epilogue**

*Lights up.*

BERTHA *in the kitchen. With a mop.*

*Shutters wide, the room full of brilliant light. And birdsong. After the rain.*

THEA *at the garden door.*

*Beat.*

THEA. I

didn't expect you to come in.

BERTHA. Nobody cancelled.

*Beat.*

It's just there are penalties, with the agency, if you don't turn up when you're booked.

I couldn't get hold of anyone and you don't want penalties.

THEA. We didn't think.

BERTHA. Course you didn't.

*Pause.*

I'm sorry.

THEA. Yeah.

*Beat.*

BERTHA. Where's your dad?

THEA. At Auntie Julie's. She likes looking after people.

BERTHA. How are you?

THEA. I can't sleep.

I walk all the time. I walk all the way from town and just walk and walk. I came out onto a hill and looked down and I could see this house in the morning.

From up there it looked

lovely.

*Beat.*

I saw a car in the drive so I came back. It must have been your /

BERTHA. Thea.

Why are you here?

THEA *goes into the sitting room. Tries to take down The General's portrait.*

Do you need help?

THEA. It's heavy…

BERTHA *goes to help her.*

BERTHA. You got it? Okay, and lift…

*Together they take down The General.*

THEA. Thanks.

THEA *half-carries, half-drags The General back into the kitchen.*

BERTHA *follows.*

BERTHA. What are you going to do with it?

THEA. Burn it.

Drown it.

Shoot it.

*Beat.*

Kill it somehow anyway.

You have to, the past, to be free.

*Pause.*

BERTHA. Is there anything else?

THEA. Else?

BERTHA. It's just I've my kids to pick up from school and there's the mopping to finish /

THEA. The thing is.

*Beat.*

It's a bit awkward. But I don't think we're going to live here. And Auntie Julie's house is really small, just a bungalow –

I guess I'm saying that, in terms of penalties. You're released from your contract.

*Beat.*

Sorry.

BERTHA. You have to go through the agency. You can do it online. There's a form you fill out and you can say nice things about me so they don't think I did anything wrong.

THEA. I'll say really nice things. Is there anything /

BERTHA. Punctual. Tidy appearance. Hard-working. Polite and friendly, but not chatty. Thorough and professional knowledge of cleaning materials. Respectful of your personal space.

THEA. I'll say all that.

*Beat.*

It's just.

He only bought it for her and /

BERTHA. You know she hated it?

   This house.

   *Beat.*

   Or maybe she just hated herself.

THEA. It wasn't like that.

   Brack's confident they'll return a verdict of accidental
   death /

BERTHA. Accidental?

THEA. Dad did tell her. He told her over and over not to play
   with those guns.

   *Beat.*

BERTHA. 'Cause I guess it's not like she had any reason.

THEA. No. She had everything. Really.

   *Silence.*

BERTHA. It's sort of quiet now isn't it?

   The house.

   *Beat.*

   *Exit* THEA, *dragging The General with her.*

   BERTHA *returns to her mopping.*

   *Lights down slow to blackout*

   *as quietly*

   *methodically*

   *she cleans up the mess.*

   *End.*

# CHICHESTER FESTIVAL THEATRE

Chichester Festival Theatre is one of the UK's flagship theatres, renowned for the exceptionally high standard of its productions as well as its work with the community and young people. Situated in a cathedral city in West Sussex between the South Downs and the sea, the Festival Theatre's bold thrust stage design makes it one of England's most striking playhouses – equally suited to epic drama and musicals. Its studio theatre, the Minerva, is particularly noted for premieres of new work alongside intimate revivals.

The annual Festival season runs from April to November, during which productions originated at Chichester reach an audience of over 230,000. Year-round programming continues through the winter with the Theatre presenting high-class touring productions, as well as a traditional Christmas show mounted by the renowned Chichester Festival Youth Theatre.

Recent transfers from Chichester (as originating producer) include *Caroline, Or Change* (London's Hampstead Theatre and the West End's Playhouse Theatre 2018/19); Ian McKellen in *King Lear*, which transferred to the West End's Noël Coward Theatre in 2018 and was broadcast to cinemas internationally by NT Live; and Daniel Evans's production of *Quiz*, a new play by James Graham, which also transferred to the West End's Noël Coward Theatre in 2018. Laura Wade's new play *The Watsons*, adapted from the unfinished novel by Jane Austen, will run at the Menier Chocolate Factory from 20 September – 16 November 2019.

Rooted firmly in its community, the Theatre runs a Learning, Education and Participation (LEAP) programme that is a beacon of excellence and inspiration to its local audience, as well as being home to one of the country's largest youth theatres with over 800 members.

For more information, visit cft.org.uk

Chairman                 Sir William Castell
Executive Director       Kathy Bourne
Artistic Director        Daniel Evans

# Headlong

**Headlong is one of the most ambitious and exciting theatre companies in the UK, creating exhilarating contemporary theatre: a provocative mix of innovative new writing, reimagined classics and influential twentieth century plays that illuminate our world.**

We make bold, groundbreaking productions with some of the UK's finest artists. We take these industry-leading, award-winning shows around the country and beyond, in theatres and online, attracting new audiences of all ages and backgrounds. We engage as deeply as we can with these communities and this helps us become better at what we do.

Our productions have included *All My Sons* (Old Vic); *Richard III* (Bristol Old Vic/UK tour); *Mother Courage and Her Children* (Manchester Royal Exchange); *Meek* (Traverse/UK tour); *This House* (Chichester Festival Theatre/West End/UK tour); *People, Places & Things* (NT/West End/UK tour/New York); *Labour of Love* (Noël Coward); *The House They Grew Up In* (Chichester Festival Theatre); *Junkyard* (Bristol Old Vic/Theatr Clwyd/Rose Theatre, Kingston); *Pygmalion* (UK tour); *Boys Will Be Boys* (Bush); *Observe the Sons of Ulster Marching Towards the Somme* (international tour); *1984* (UK and international tour/West End); *The Nether* (Royal Court/West End); *The Glass Menagerie* (UK tour); *American Psycho* (Almeida/Broadway); *Chimerica* (Almeida/West End) and *Enron* (UK tour/West End/ Broadway).

Many thanks to our Hedonists: Nick Archdale, Ginny & Humphrey Battcock, Neil and Sarah Brener, Scott Delman, Cas and Philip Donald, Annabel Duncan-Smith, Nick Hern, Nicky Jones, Jack Keenan, Victoria Leggett, Kate Mallinckrodt, Stephen Marquardt & Deborah Shaw, Caroline Maude, Beth and Ian Mill QC, Neil & Shelly Mitchell, Donna Munday, Georgia Oetker, Rob O'Rahilly, Robin Paxton, Prasanna Puwaranajah, Jon & NoraLee Sedmak, Jack Thorne and Lesley Wan.

Headlong would also like to thank Arts Council England, The Backstage Trust, The Buffini Chao Foundation, The Cockayne Foundation (a donor-advised fund managed by the London Community Foundation), The Esmée Fairbairn Foundation and The Garfield Weston Foundation for their generous support.

**Headlong.co.uk | @HeadlongTheatre**

West End cast for *People, Places and Things*, 2016 Photo: Johan Persson

# THE LOWRY

The Lowry is an arts organisation based in Salford, Greater Manchester. Home to two galleries, three theatres and Pier Eight bar and restaurant, the venue welcomes more than 830,000 people per year. Working with more than 350 artists and companies it stages more than a 1,000 performances a year.

As a registered charity, The Lowry is committed to using visual and performing arts to enrich people's lives through a diverse programme of performance, events and activities and work with local communities and young people.

Named after the artist LS Lowry, the building is home to the world's largest public collection of his works and has a permanent exhibition on display year-round. The gallery also presents an exciting programme of work by contemporary artists throughout the year.

Alongside a programme of work by acclaimed international artists and companies, The Lowry is committed to commissioning exciting, relevant and contemporary productions as part of its biennial Week 53 Festival. In addition, as part of The Lowry's Artist Development Programme, the organisation provides bespoke pathways that aims to nurture artists and companies at different stages in their practice allowing them to present bold, dynamic and innovative work.

Find out more at **thelowry.com**